Virtual Reality Blue

Create compelling VR experiences for mobile and desktop

Charles Palmer
John Williamson

BIRMINGHAM - MUMBAI

Virtual Reality Blueprints

Commissioning Editor: Amarabha Banerjee
Acquisition Editor: Larissa Pinto
Content Development Editor: Aditi Gour
Technical Editor: Harshal Kadam
Copy Editor: Safis Editing
Project Coordinator: Hardik Bhinde
Proofreader: Safis Editing
Indexer: Pratik Shirodkar
Graphics: Jason Monteiro
Production Coordinator: Aparna Bhagat

First published: February 2018

Production reference: 1260218

Published by Packt Publishing Ltd.
Livery Place
35 Livery Street
Birmingham
B3 2PB, UK.

ISBN 978-1-78646-298-5

www.packtpub.com

`mapt.io`

Mapt is an online digital library that gives you full access to over 5,000 books and videos, as well as industry leading tools to help you plan your personal development and advance your career. For more information, please visit our website.

Why subscribe?

- Spend less time learning and more time coding with practical eBooks and Videos from over 4,000 industry professionals

- Improve your learning with Skill Plans built especially for you

- Get a free eBook or video every month

- Mapt is fully searchable

- Copy and paste, print, and bookmark content

PacktPub.com

Did you know that Packt offers eBook versions of every book published, with PDF and ePub files available? You can upgrade to the eBook version at `www.PacktPub.com` and as a print book customer, you are entitled to a discount on the eBook copy. Get in touch with us at `service@packtpub.com` for more details.

At `www.PacktPub.com`, you can also read a collection of free technical articles, sign up for a range of free newsletters, and receive exclusive discounts and offers on Packt books and eBooks.

Foreword

I first had the privilege of working with Charles Palmer in 2002 when I joined the Entertainment Technology Center at Carnegie Mellon University. Both Charles and I were lucky enough to work with virtual reality pioneer Randy Pausch, whom you might know from his famous book and video entitled *The Last Lecture*. Randy was a great believer in the future of virtual reality. He really believed, like I do, that it is the most important development in computer technology to happen in our lifetime. Randy devoted the majority of his career to figuring out how to best use VR to create incredible experiences, and one way he did this was by creating a class called Building Virtual Worlds, which challenged students to use bleeding edge VR technologies to create powerful and innovative experiences. The central philosophy of the class was that there was no time to sit around theorizing about what might work—the best way to learn about virtual reality is to jump right in! Fifteen years later, Randy is no longer with us, but the class goes on, and though the technology has advanced, we still jump right in!

Of course, jumping in with the support of an advanced graduate program is one thing, and jumping in on your own is something else again! Fortunately for you, Charles Palmer and Producer/Writer John Williamson have crafted this wonderful book, which provides everything you need to get started crafting your own innovative virtual worlds right away. Great virtual worlds are immersive, and so is this book! Whether you have access to an Oculus Rift, a Gear VR headset, or even just Google Cardboard, this book provides everything you need to jump right in and get started.

VR will change the way we live, work, and play. As happened with electricity, the internet, and smart phones, one day we will all look back and wonder how we ever got along without it. As Willy Wonka's golden ticket proclaims, *In your wildest dreams, you could not imagine the marvelous surprises that await you! So why wait? Virtual Reality Blueprints* is a wonderful gateway to hands-on VR development. You will find that creating great VR can be hard work, but with the help of this *Virtual Reality Blueprints*, it will also be a tremendous amount of fun, and as Randy once told us, *Never, ever underestimate the importance of having fun.*

Jesse Schell
Distinguished Professor of the Practice of Entertainment Technology,

Carnegie Mellon University,
CEO, Schell Games,

February, 2018

Contributors

About the authors

Charles Palmer is an associate professor and executive director at Harrisburg University. He oversees the design and development of new and emerging technologies, chairs the undergraduate Interactive Media program, and advises students on applied projects in AR/VR, game development, mobile computing, web design, social media, and gamification. He is also a happy husband, father, award-winning web designer, international speaker, and 3D printing enthusiast.

Thank you to Paula and Madison for believing in me more than myself, Susan Henderson, Saeeda Hafiz, and Jesse Schell for their unwitting inspiration, and students past and present for providing an endless source of motivation.
To my HU and ETC families, especially Ralph, Don, Eric, and Bili, thanks for taking a chance and being supportive.
Special thanks to Tyler Batts, who's programming skills brought this project to life.

John Williamson has worked in VR since 1995. As a producer/designer, he has shipped over three dozen games (America's Army, Hawken, SAW, and Spec Ops) in nearly every genre (RTS, FPS, Arcade, Simulation, Survival Horror) on nearly every platform (iOS, Android, Wii, PlayStation, Xbox, web, PC, and VR). He is also an award-winning filmmaker and has taught game design at DigiPen and Harrisburg University. Now, he works in VR, creating immersive training for a wide range of high-consequence trainers for the US Air Force, Army, and NASA.

I would like to thank my wife and daughter for their patience, Dr. Tom Furness and Capt. T.K. Treadwell for their VR inspiration, my parents for giving the option to explore games and VR for a living at an early age, and my students for helping keep me young.

About the reviewer

Gianni Rosagallina is an Italian senior SW engineer and architect, focused on emerging technologies AI and VR's/AR's since 2013. Currently, he works in Deltatre's Innovation Lab, prototyping solutions for next-gen sport experiences and business services. Besides that, he has over 10 years of certified experience as a consultant on Microsoft and .NET technologies (IoT, cloud, and desktop/mobile apps). Since 2011, he has been awarded Microsoft MVP in Windows Development. He has been a Pluralsight author since 2013 and speaks at national and international conferences.

Packt is searching for authors like you

If you're interested in becoming an author for Packt, please visit `authors.packtpub.com` and apply today. We have worked with thousands of developers and tech professionals, just like you, to help them share their insight with the global tech community. You can make a general application, apply for a specific hot topic that we are recruiting an author for, or submit your own idea.

Table of Contents

Preface

In Q3 of 2017, the **virtual reality (VR)** hardware industry achieved a new milestone. After years of slow adoption rates and lagging sales, manufacturers sold 1 million VR headsets. This achievement astounded many tech writers who had predicted that the technology would be relegated to early adopters and the techno-curious. However, the industry is finally seeing its greatest amount of traction since the release of the modern consumer headsets. Also, this adoption is ushering in a boom for VR developers. With lower headset costs and a strong consumer market, industries across the globe are investing in VR titles. This is not just entertainment companies; industries such as manufacturing, healthcare, retail sales, and education are leading the charge to explore new ventures and uses for VR technologies.

Just look at employment companies such as Glassdoor, Indeed, and Monster. New job postings for VR developers are emerging daily in every US tech market, from New York to Houston TX to Redmond WA. VR development skills are in hot demand.

In this book, we offer a practical, project-based approach to VR development. Using four approachable but thought-provoking concepts, we teach the specifics of implementing VR projects using the Unity development platform. Each project starts as a step-by-step guide, but also includes discussions on VR best practices, design choices, technical challenges, and guidance for the improvement and implementation of your own solutions.

Our hope is that you will walk away with a new set of skills, an appreciation for VR development, and ideas for creating rich, immersive experiences using the Unity platform.

Who this book is for

Have you ever wanted to build your own VR experience? Do you have an idea for creating an immersive environment? Do you have access to a VR headset? If any of these questions are true, then this book is for you. The content here is intended for programmers and non-programmers alike. Some knowledge of the Unity game engine is required, but even novice developers should be able to follow along and adapt to the step-by-step tutorials.

What this book covers

Chapter 1, *The Past, Present, and Future of VR*, provides a detailed introduction to the virtual reality platform, from its early beginnings in the late 1700s to the hardware devices of today. This chapter looks at the persistence of vision, stereoscopy, and haptic feedback combined with bridging the virtual and physical worlds.

Chapter 2, *Building a Solar System for Google Cardboard*, is a simple starting project using the Trappist-1 Solar System as a backdrop for introducing VR development to the novice user.

Chapter 3, *Building an Image Gallery System for the Gear VR*, uses virtual field trips, the cornerstone of VR titles, to illustrate how to construct virtual sets. This chapter also outlines the planning process for user engagement. This is another introductory project intended for the novice user.

Chapter 4, *Adding User Interactions to the Virtual Gallery Project*, makes the case that the key to VR immersion is user interaction. In this chapter, we introduce the subject of immersion by expanding the Image Gallery to accept user input. A series of controller scripts are constructed for image and gallery selection within VR spaces. This project is geared to the Intermediate Unity Developer, but the instructions and methodology are structured for all skill levels.

Chapter 5, *Fighting Zombies on the Oculus Rift*, examines the first-person shooter genre. Shooter games, both first- and third-person, have been firmly cemented as the top game genre for well over a decade. Part 1 of the Zombie shooter project covers constructing an environment, implementing a raycaster system, and using state machines to control prefab animation. Along the way, we also identify techniques for optimizing VR experiences.

Chapter 6, *Scripting Zombies for the Oculus Rift*, covers the second part of the Zombie shooter. Here, we explain and construct scripts for controlling zombie and player interactions. Some Unity scripting experience is expected, but detailed instructions are available for novice users.

Chapter 7, *Carnival Midway Games — Part 1*, is the final project of the book. Together, we will construct two mini games commonly found at community carnivals. Part 1 covers building the environment, discussing level design techniques, and planning the teleportation system.

Chapter 8, *Carnival Midway Games — Part 2*, provides instructions for adding UI elements, scripting various game objects, and finalizing the project. As a final task, the reader should extend beyond the content presented here, adding Asset Store items or custom game objects to complete the carnival mood.

`Appendix A`, *VR Hardware Roundup,* is a catalog of the current VR headsets. It provides product details, specifications, and price comparisons.

`Appendix B`, *VR Terms and Definitions,* provides ancillary VR terminology for those looking for a deeper understanding of the concepts covered in this book. This appendix also includes best practices for input, movement, and designing user experiences.

To get the most out of this book

Before getting started with the projects outlined in this book, you will need a few things. The first is a Mac or PC computer that meets the Unity 3D system requirements. Visit `https://unity3d.com/unity/system-requirements` to confirm that your computer can run the software.

This book uses the free version of the Unity 3D game engine. If you are not familiar with the engine, visit `https://unity3d.com/learn/tutorials/topics/interface-essentials` for an introduction on the interface and basic game objects. The engine is constantly under development for improvements and feature releases. New patches are announced monthly, and major version releases appear two to three times a year. With this ever-changing nature, readers should install the latest version of Unity and visit `https://unity3d.com/unity/roadmap` to review any updates to the VR toolset.

Although a computer is required to develop each project, a VR headset is still needed to fully test the environments. We designed these tutorials for the Google Cardboard (Project: Trappist-1 Solar System), Samsung Gear VR (Project: Image Gallery), and Oculus Rift (Project: Zombie Shooter, Carnival Midway). However, the concepts are universal and with minor adjustments, the projects can be adapted to other devices as well.

Each hardware platform requires a **Software Development Kit (SDK)** or custom Unity package to facilitate communication between Unity and the VR device. Instructions for installation can be found at the beginning of each project. It is also important to check for software compatibility with your installed version of Unity. This can be done at the download site or in the VR Device section of Unity at `https://docs.unity3d.com/Manual/VRDevices.html`.

Download the example code files

You can download the example code files for this book from your account at
`www.packtpub.com`. If you purchased this book elsewhere, you can visit
`www.packtpub.com/support` and register to have the files emailed directly to you.

You can download the code files by following these steps:

1. Log in or register at `www.packtpub.com`.
2. Select the **SUPPORT** tab.
3. Click on **Code Downloads & Errata**.
4. Enter the name of the book in the **Search** box and follow the onscreen
   instructions.

Once the file is downloaded, please make sure that you unzip or extract the folder using the
latest version of:

- WinRAR/7-Zip for Windows
- Zipeg/iZip/UnRarX for Mac
- 7-Zip/PeaZip for Linux

The code bundle for the book is also hosted on GitHub at `https://github.com/
PacktPublishing/Virtual-Reality-Blueprints`**</span>**. We also have other code bundles
from our rich catalog of books and videos available at `https://github.com/
PacktPublishing/`. Check them out!

Download the color images

We also provide a PDF file that has color images of the screenshots/diagrams used in this
book. You can download it here: `http://www.packtpub.com/sites/default/files/
downloads/VirtualRealityBlueprints_ColorImages.pdf`.

Conventions used

There are a number of text conventions used throughout this book.

`CodeInText`: Indicates code words in text, database table names, folder names, filenames,
file extensions, pathnames, dummy URLs, user input, and Twitter handles. Here is an
example: "Finally, we will keep the project organized by dragging the `OrbitController`'s
icon to the `Scripts` folder."

A block of code is set as follows:

```
public Transform orbitPivot;
public float orbitSpeed;
public float rotationSpeed;
public float planetRadius;
public float distFromStar;
```

Bold: Indicates a new term, an important word, or words that you see onscreen. For example, words in menus or dialog boxes appear in the text like this. Here is an example: "Create a new sphere using **GameObject | 3D Object | Sphere**."

 Warnings or important notes appear like this.

 Tips and tricks appear like this.

Get in touch

Feedback from our readers is always welcome.

General feedback: Email `feedback@packtpub.com` and mention the book title in the subject of your message. If you have questions about any aspect of this book, please email us at `questions@packtpub.com`.

Errata: Although we have taken every care to ensure the accuracy of our content, mistakes do happen. If you have found a mistake in this book, we would be grateful if you would report this to us. Please visit `www.packtpub.com/submit-errata`, selecting your book, clicking on the Errata Submission Form link, and entering the details.

Piracy: If you come across any illegal copies of our works in any form on the Internet, we would be grateful if you would provide us with the location address or website name. Please contact us at `copyright@packtpub.com` with a link to the material.

If you are interested in becoming an author: If there is a topic that you have expertise in and you are interested in either writing or contributing to a book, please visit `authors.packtpub.com`.

Reviews

Please leave a review. Once you have read and used this book, why not leave a review on the site that you purchased it from? Potential readers can then see and use your unbiased opinion to make purchase decisions, we at Packt can understand what you think about our products, and our authors can see your feedback on their book. Thank you!

For more information about Packt, please visit packtpub.com.

1

The Past, Present, and Future of VR

This book is designed to serve as a hands-on introduction to virtual reality, commonly known as simply VR. The book includes a brief history of the technology, some definitions of popular terms, as well as best practices to stave off motion sickness and ensure your trackers are working perfectly.

In the following chapters, you will begin creating your very own virtual worlds which you can explore using your mobile device or **Head Mounted Display (HMD)**. Unity 3D will be used for all projects. Unity is a flexible and powerful video game engine used to create some of your favorite video games, such as Hearthstone, Cities Skylines, Kerbal Space Program, Cuphead, Super Hot, and Monument Valley.

The Virtual Worlds you will be creating in Unity include:

- **Image Gallery**: A Virtual Art Gallery/Museum where you get to decide what hangs on the walls in this Samsung Gear VR project.
- **Solar System**: Ignore the rules of time and physics as you travel through a model of the solar system in Google Cardboard.
- **Zombie Shooter**: The only good zombie is a dead one—wait, an undead one? Anyway, you'll shoot them in the Oculus Rift.
- **Carnival Games**: The only thing missing from these realistic VR carnival games is the smell of fried pickles.

Additionally, you will cover Unity development topics, such as:

- System requirements
- Scripting in Unity

- User interaction in VR
- Building VR environments
- Equirectangular images
- Improving performance
- The Samsung Gear VR workflow process
- The Oculus Rift workflow process
- Combating VR sickness

The history of virtual reality

The development of virtual reality has been driven by the confluence of three improvements to display technologies:

- **Field of View**: the size of the area that we can see
- **Stereoscopic 3D**: the depth cue from viewing the world from two different horizontally separated viewpoints
- **Interactivity**: the ability to change the virtual environment in real time

In this chapter, we are going to illustrate the history of virtual reality and how earlier designs have served as inspiration for today, even a few older ideas that we have not quite duplicated with our current generation of VR hardware.

We will investigate the following:

- 19th century panoramic paintings
- Cycloramas and Sensoramas
- NASA Moon Landing Simulators
- Nintendo Powerglove
- Hasbro Toaster

Static 2D images, whether paintings or photographs, are poor representations of reality. As such, people have striven to enhance their images, to make them more realistic and immersive since the first flickering shadows added motion to cave paintings 20,000 years ago. Simple puppets added motion and then depth. More complex solutions were designed: motion and audio effects were added to Greek and Roman temples to give a complete sensory experience. Doors would open without apparent human interaction, thunder would rumble overhead, and fountains would dance: all designed to create an augmented experience beyond simple static statues and paintings.

Through the looking glass

Perspective, a great example of the intersection between art and math, allowed us to accurately trace the world as we see it. Artists learned to mix paints to create the illusion of translucency in pigments. Magicians were able to use persistence of vision to create illusions and children's toys that would one day lead to moving pictures and create *holograms* of dead pop stars:

Magic lanterns are an extension of the Camera Obscura and can be traced back to the 17th century. Rather than using the light from the sun, as a Camera Obscura did, an artificial light was used: first candlelight, then limelight, then electricity. The light was shown through a painted glass plate which was projected on the wall, very much like a slide projector (or even video projector). The images could be scrolled, giving the illusion of motion, or two images could be alternated, giving the illusion of animation. The simple technology of magic lanterns was popular for over 200 years, up until the 1920s when moving pictures finally dethroned them:

Making a static image dance

Zoetropes: Several designs and children's toys experimented with the idea of rapidly presenting a series of static images to create the illusion of motion. But not until 18-year-old William Lincoln presented his design to Milton Bradley did the design take off. The trick was to place slits in the viewing device so that the images would only be seen briefly and not continuously. This *persistence of vision*, the fact that an image remains visible after it is removed, is what allows movies, a series of still images, to be seen in motion:

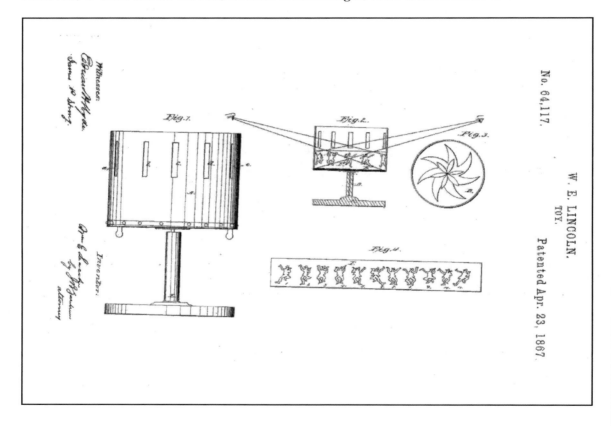

The bigger the better – panoramic paintings

Along the way, artists began to experiment with large-scale paintings, that were so large they would eclipse the viewer's entire field of view, enhancing the illusion that one was not simply in the theater or gallery, but on location. The paintings would be curved in a semi-circle to enhance the effect, the first of which may have been created in 1791 in England by Robert Barker. They proved so financially successful that over 120 different Panorama installations were reported between 1793 and 1863 in London alone. This wide field-of-view solution used to draw audiences would be repeated by Hollywood in the 1950s with Cinerama, a projection system that required three synchronized cameras and three synchronized projectors to create an ultra-wide field of view. This was again improved on by Circle Vision 360 and IMAX over the years:

For a brief period of time, these large-scale paintings were taken even a step further with two enhancements. The first was to shorten the field of view to a narrower fixed point, but to make the image very long—hundreds of meters long, in fact. This immense painting would be slowly unrolled to an audience, often through a window to add an extra layer of depth, typically and with a narrated tour guide, thus giving the illusion that they were looking out of a steamboat window, floating down the Mississippi (or the Nile) as their guide lectured about the flora and fauna that drifted by.

As impressive as this technology was, it had first been used centuries earlier by the Chinese, though on a smaller scale:

A version of this mechanism was used in the 1899 Broadway production of Ben-Hur, which ran for 21 years and sold over 20 million tickets. One of the advertising posters is shown here. The actual result was a little different:

A giant screen of the Roman coliseum would scroll behind two chariots, pulled by live horse while fans blew dust, giving the impression of being on the chariot track in the middle of the race. This technique would be used later in rear-screen projections for film special effects, and even to help land a man on the moon, as we shall see:

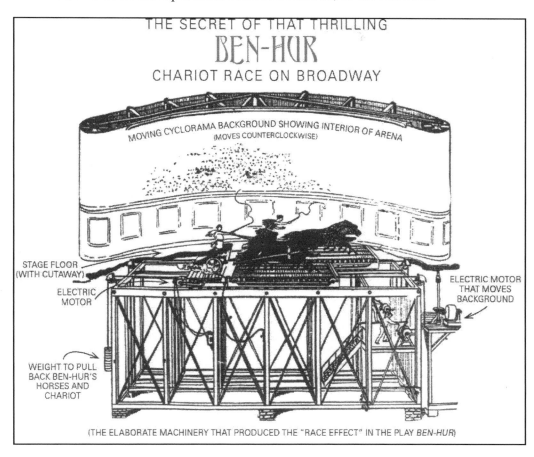

(THE ELABORATE MACHINERY THAT PRODUCED THE "RACE EFFECT" IN THE PLAY *BEN-HUR*)

The next step was to make the painting rotate a full 360 degrees and place the viewer in the center. Later versions would add 3D sculptures, then animated lights and positional scripted audio, to further enhance the experience and blur the line between realism and 2D painting. Several of these can still be seen in the US, including the Battle of Gettysburg Cyclorama, in Gettysburg, Pennsylvania.

Stereoscopic viewers

Stereoscopic vision is an important evolutionary trait with a set of trade-offs. Nearly all land-based, mammalian predators have forward facing eyes for stereoscopic vision. This allows them to detect objects that may be camouflaged or helps them sort depth to be able to know where to attack. However, this gives predators a narrow field of view, and they are unable to detect movement behind them. Nearly all prey animals have eyes on the sides of their heads for a far wider field of view, allowing them to detect predators from the side and rear.

Artificial stereoscopic images where first created in 1838 when Charles Wheatstone created his stereoscopic viewer, built with mirrors. Fortunately, the invention of the photographic camera occurred nearly simultaneously, as drawing two nearly identical images, separated by just 6.5 centimeters, is a very difficult task:

Brewster improved on the design just 10 years later. But, it was Poet and Dean of Harvard Medical School, Oliver Wendell Holmes Sr., whose 1861 redesign made it a phenomenon. His belief in stereo-photography as an educational tool was such that he purposely did not patent it. This lowered the cost and ensured it would be used as widely as possible. There was scarcely a Victorian parlor that did not have a Holmes stereo viewer. This is the design most frequently associated with stereoscopic antiques, and remained the most popular design until View Master took over in 1939:

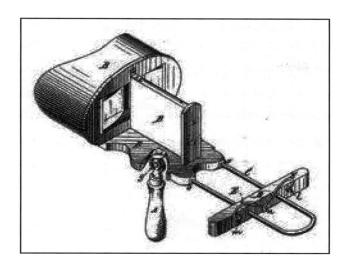

Stereoscopic media requires that two, near-identical images be presented, one to each eye. However, each solution varies in the way they ensure the eye sees only the image intended for it: the left eye sees only the left image and the right eye sees only the right image.

In early stereoscopic displays, and all VR HMDs today, this is done simply by using separate lenses directed at each eye, ensuring that each eye sees only the image designed for it. From the Viewmaster to the Vive, the same basic technique is used. This works perfectly for one viewer at a time.

But, if you want to show a 3D movie to a crowd, you need different techniques to ensure that there is no *crosstalk*. That is, you still want the left eye to see only the left image and the right eye only the right image. With 3D movies, there were a handful of different techniques, each with advantages and disadvantages.

The most affordable option is the one often used for 3D comic books: anaglyph 3D. Typically, this involves Red/Cyan lenses (though sometimes Green/Yellow). The left image would be printed in Red ink, the right image in Cyan ink. The Red lens would block the Cyan, the Cyan lens would block the Red. The effect does work, though there is always some *crosstalk* when some of each image is still visible by the opposite eye.

Polarized 3D allowed for full-color images to be used, using a technique such as anaglyph glasses. One set of polarized light would pass through one lens, but the orthogonal polarized light would be blocked. This could even be used in print images, though at a significant cost increase over anaglyph 3D. Polarized 3D is the type most commonly used in 3D movies today.

Active shutters were, at first, a mechanical shutter that would block each eye in sync with the movie, which would only show one eye at a time. Later, these mechanical shutters were replaced with **Liquid Crystal Displays (LCD)** that would block out most (but not all) light. This is the 3D technique used in the Sega 3D system, and was also used in some IMAX 3D systems:

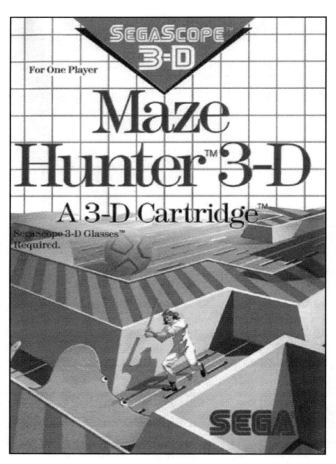

There were many other 3D techniques: volumetric displays built with lasers and mirrors or light arrays, Chromadepth, and holograms. But none were as successful as the techniques previously discussed.

Real, interactive holograms exist only in science fiction. The *Holograms* of Tupac and Michael Jackson are actually based on a 19th century magic trick called *Pepper's Ghost*, and are simply 2D images projected onto a pane of glass. The *Holographic* images of the HoloLens are also not real holograms, as they too use a version of Pepper's Ghost, where the images above are projected down into a set of semi-transparent optics:

Lenticular displays deserve to be mentioned for two reasons. First, they allow the user to see 3D without the use of glasses. Second, even though the technology has been around for at least 75 years, most people are familiar with lenticular displays because of the Nintendo 3DS. A lenticular display cuts the image into very thin, alternating vertical strips, one set for the left eye, one set for the right eye. Each eye is prevented from seeing the other eye's images though the use of a parallax barrier.

Why stop at just sight and sound? – Smell o' Vision and Sensorama

While this generation of VR has not (yet) added the olfactory sense to their set of outputs, this does not mean that older systems have not tried.

Movies tried to add the sense of smell in 1960 with the movie *Scent of Mystery*. At specific times in the movie, smells were sprayed into the audience. Some theatergoers complained that the smells were overpowering, while others complained they could not smell them at all. But everyone agreed that the movie, even with Elizabeth Taylor, was not worth seeing, and this technology quietly faded away:

Morton Heilig built the Sensorama in 1962. Only a single viewer at a time could experience the short films, but the viewers were exposed to all the senses: Stereoscopic 3D, smells, vibration, wind in the hair, and stereo sound. Today, *4D* movies at many major theme parks are its closest relatives.

Heilig did attempt to create a large audience version of his immersive films, which included elements from Sensorama and the Cyclorama. He called this the Telesphere. The large field of view, stereoscopic 3D images, and vibrations were designed to create an immersive experience.

Link Trainers and Apollo

World War One took aviation from flights of hundreds of meters to flights measured in hundreds of kilometers. Early flight trainers were no more than barrels on ropes. Edward Link saw the potential for growth in aviation and the need for trained pilots to fly these more complex aircraft. The complexity of new planes would require a new level of fidelity in training systems, and the number of new pilots could not meet demand with current techniques.

This was brought to the forefront when 12 pilots were killed in training in less than three months. Link took his knowledge of building pump organs and created analog flight simulators designed to teach flight by instruments. There were no graphics of any kind and no scrolling landscapes, and the pilots were enclosed in a darkened covered cockpit. The trainers would respond accurately to the pilot's stick and rudder inputs and the little boxes would pitch and roll a few degrees. Link Trainers would add small stubby wings and a tail, making them look like the children's rides outside grocery stores in the 1950s, but over 500,000 pilots were trained with them.

For the Apollo program, true digital computers were used in simulators, but the computers were not powerful enough to display graphics. The computers displayed the simple analog readouts of the computers in the capsules. To simulate the view from the capsule, large three-dimensional models and paintings were built of the moon and space vehicles. The moon was scrolled under a Closed-Circuit TV Camera:

This was not unlike the scrolling panoramic paintings used a hundred years earlier. The video feed from the camera was sent to a special *infinity optical display system* mounted in the simulator capsule, which had a wide field of view of 110 degrees. As the astronaut trained in the simulator, the movement of his joystick was fed into the position of the cameras, changing the images projected in real time. This system featured wide field of view and interactivity, but not stereoscopic 3D images (though the life-sized cockpit model they looked through would add binocular depth to the presentation).

Interactivity and True HMDs

In this section we will conduct a quick overview of the evolution of Head Mounted Displays, including how they displayed their images and what head tracking technologies they used.

1960 – TelesphereMask

Morton Heilig patented one of the first functioning HMDs in 1960. While it did not have any head tracking and was designed exclusively for his stereoscopic 3D movies, the images from the patent look remarkably familiar to our designs 50 years later:

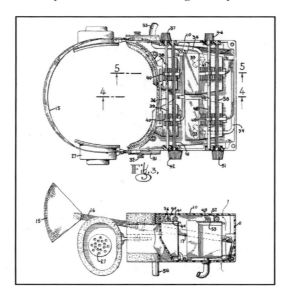

1961 – Headsight

This was a remote-viewing HMD designed for safely inspecting dangerous situations. This was also the first interactive HMD. The user could change the direction of the cameras from the live video feed by rotating their head, seeing the view angles update in real time. This was one step closer to immersive environments and telepresence.

1968 – Teleyeglasses

Hugo Gernsback bridged the gap between the sections on Science Fiction and HMD Design. Hugo was a prolific publisher, publishing over 50 hobbyist magazines based around science, technology, and science fiction. The *Hugo* awards for science fiction are named after him. While readers loved him, his reputation among contemporary writers was less than flattering.

Hugo not only published science fiction, he himself wrote about futurism, from color television, to cities on the moon, to farming in space. In 1968, he debuted a wireless HMD, called the *Teleyglasses*, constructed from twin **Cathode-ray tubes (CRT)** with *rabbit ear* antenna.

1965 – The Ultimate Display

Ivan Sutherland wrote about the Ultimate Display, a computer system that could simulate reality to the point where one could not differentiate between reality and simulation. The concept included haptic inputs and an HMD, the first complete definition of what Star Trek would call the Holodeck. We still do not have high-fidelity haptic feedback, though prototypes do exist.

> *The ultimate display would, of course, be a room within which the computer can control the existence of matter. A chair displayed in such a room would be good enough to sit in. Handcuffs displayed in such a room would be confining, and a bullet displayed in such a room would be fatal. With appropriate programming such a display could literally be the Wonderland into which Alice walked.*

> *- Ivan Sutherland*

1968 – Sword of Damocles

In 1968, Sutherland demonstrated an HMD with interactive computer graphics: the first true HMD. It was too large and heavy to be comfortably worn, so it was suspended from the ceiling. This gave it its *name* (Damocles had a sword suspended over his head by a single hair, to show him the perilous nature of those in power).

The computer-generated images were interactive: as the user turned their head, the images would update accordingly. But, given the computer processing power of the time, the images were simple white vector-line drawings against a black background. The rotation of the head was tracked electromechanically through gears (unlike today's HMDs, which use gyroscopes and light sensors), which no doubt added to the weight. Sutherland would go on to co-found *Evans* and *Southerland*, a leading computer image processing company in the 1970s and 1980s:

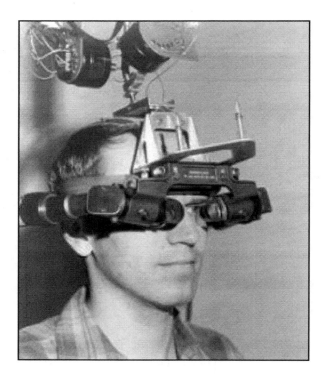

1968 – The mother of all demos

While this demo did not have an HMD, it did contain a demo of virtually every system used in computers today: the Mouse, Lightpen, Networking with audio, video, collaborative word processing, hypertext, and more. Fortunately, the videos of the event are online and well worth a look.

1969 – Virtual Cockpit/Helmet Mounted Sight

Dr. Tom Furness began working on HMDs for the US Air Force in 1967, moving from Heads Up Displays, to Helmet Mounted Displays, to Head Mounted Displays in 1969. At first, the idea was just to be able to take some of the mental load off of the pilot and allow them to focus on the most important instruments. Later, this evolved into linking the head of the pilot to the gun turret, allowing them to fire where they looked. The current F-35 Glass Cockpit HMD can be traced directly to his work. In a Glass Cockpit or even Glass Tank, the pilot or driver is able to *see through* their plane or tank via an HMD, giving them a complete unobstructed view of the battlefield through sensors and cameras mounted in the hull. His Retinal Display Systems, which do away with pixels by writing directly on the eye with lasers, is possibly similar to the solution of Magic Leap.

1969 – Artificial Reality

Myron Kruegere was a virtual reality computer artist who is credited with coming up with the term *Artificial Reality* to describe several of his interactive, computer-powered art installations: GLOWFLOW, METAPLAY, PSYCHIC SPACE, and VIDEOPLACE. If you visited a hands-on science museum from the 1970s through the 1990s, you no doubt experienced variations of his video/computer interactions. Several web and phone camera apps have similar features built-in now.

1995 – CAVE

Cave Automatic Virtual Environment (CAVE) is a self-referential acronym. It was the first collaborative space where multiple users could interact in virtual space. The systems used at least three, though sometimes more, stereoscopic 3D projectors covering at least three walls a room. Creating life-sized 3D computer images, the user could walk through them. While stereoscopic 3D projectors are inexpensive today, at the time their extremely high cost, coupled with the cost of computers to create realistic images in real time, meant CAVE systems were relegated to biomedical and automotive research facilities.

1987 – Virtual reality and VPL

Jaron Lanier coined (or popularized, depending on your sources) the term virtual reality. Jaron Lanier designed and built the first most complete commercially-available virtual reality system. It included the Dataglove and the EyePhone head-mounted display. The Dataglove would evolve into the Nintendo Powerglove. The Dataglove was able to track hand gestures through a unique trait of fiber optic cable. If you scratch a fiber optic cable, and shine light through it while it is straight, very little of the light will escape. But if you bend the scratched fiber optic cable, light will escape, and the more you bend it, the more light escapes. This light was measured and then used to calculate finger movements.

While the first generation of VR tried to use natural, gesture-based input (specifically hand), today's latest iteration of VR is, for the most part, skips hand-based input (with the exception of Leap and, to a very limited extent, HoloLens). My theory is that the new generation of VR developers grew up with a controller in their hands and were very comfortable with that input device, whereas the original set of VR designers had very little experience with a controller and that is why they felt the need to use natural input.

1989 – Nintendo Powerglove

The Nintendo Powerglove was an accessory designed to run on the **Nintendo Entertainment System (NES)**. It used a set of three ultrasonic speakers that would be mounted to a TV to track the location of the player's hand. In theory, the player could grab objects by making a fist with their hand in the glove. Tightening and relaxing the hand would change how much electrical resistance was captured, allowing the NES to register a fist or an open hand. Only two games were released for the system, though its cultural impact was far greater:

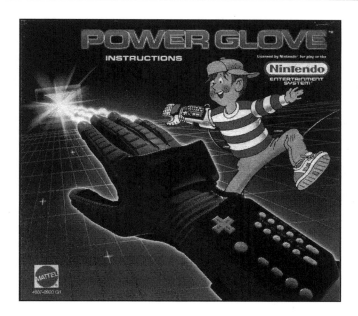

1990s – VR Explosion

In the 1990s, VR made its first foray into the mainstream. At least three PC HMDs made it to market and several console VR systems were built.

1991 – Virtuality Dactyl Nightmare

Virtuality was the first VR Experience to be publicly available in video game arcades, as the price point of the computers required to draw even these simple 3D images were well beyond what any household could afford. These experiences were even networked together for multiplayer VR interaction:

1993 – SEGA VR glasses

Sega announced the Sega VR headset for the Sega Genesis console in 1993 at the Consumer Electronics Show. The system included head tracking, stereo sound, and images drawn on two LCD screens. SEGA built four games for the system, but a high price point and lack of computer power meant the HMD never went into production:

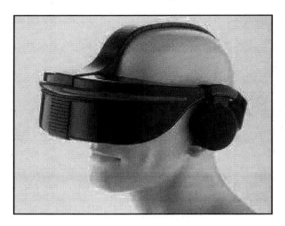

1995 – VRML – Virtual reality Markup Language

VRML is a text file format designed to link 3D worlds together, much like **Hyper Text Markup Language** (**HTML**) links pages together. Vertices, edges, surface color, UV mapped textures, and transparency for 3D polygons could be specified. Animated effects and audio could be triggered as well:

1995 – Nintendo Virtual Boy

The Nintendo Virtual Boy did not have any head tracking at all; it was a stereoscopic 3D display system that ran proprietary games that only had two colors: red and black. While several dozen games were released for it, the system was difficult to use comfortably and the experience could not be shared. The Virtual Boy was only on the market for two years:

1995 – Hasbro Toaster

Hasbro, the toy manufacturer, had missed out on the console booms of the 80s and 90s and wanted to get into that very lucrative market. They designed a CD-ROM-based system powerful enough to run VR and built a VR prototype. After a great deal of money was invested, the system was never released, though the game Night Trap was built for the system. As the game was so expensive to produce, the developers salvaged what they could and released it for the Sega CD system:

2013 – Oculus Rift

Palmer Lucky was able to leverage the never-ending demand for VR; the dramatic increase in PC processing power, the advent of low-cost, high-quality hobbyist hardware and circuit boards; the explosion of the large screen; high-resolution smart phone display, which is still the primary source of screens in HMDs and the raw power and acceptance of crowd-sourcing. This perfect storm of tech, money, ideas, enthusiasm, and execution allowed him to sell his company to Facebook for $2 billion.

Palmer deserves credit for re-creating the VR demand that has brought us Cardboard, Gear, Daydream, and HoloLens, which are all discussed in greater detail elsewhere in this book.

2014 – Google Cardboard

While Facebook invested $2 billion to bring Rift to the market, Google took a different approach. Google Cardboard is an HMD kit that contains two 40 mm focal distance lenses and a sheet of pre-folded die-cut cardboard. Rubber bands and Velcro strips are used to keep the device closed and support the user's mobile device. With a low price point, around $9.00, and simple design, VR finally made it into the hands of millions of users.

Since its initial release, knock-off brands have kept the price low and Google has developed educational materials for K-8 students across the U.S.

2015 – Samsung Gear VR

In 2005, Samsung obtained a patent to use a mobile device as a head-mounted display. This led to the release of the Gear VR in November of 2015. The Gear VR is designed to work with Samsung's flagship smartphones, with an integrated calibration wheel and trackpad for user interaction.

The Oculus-compatible Samsung device supports **Motion to Photon** (**MTP**) with latency less than 20 ms, optimized hardware and kernel, and higher-resolution rendering for the 96 degree field of view for the first three models, and 101 degree for the SM-R323 and beyond.

2018 – Magic Leap

Magic Leap is one of many unreleased HMDs, but, as it has the backing of Google to the tune of $2 billion and promises an AR experience far beyond that of the HoloLens, the system deserves to be mentioned, even though there is little to write about beyond some *proof of concept* videos.

Summary

This look at the science and technical history of virtual reality now prepares us to build new VR experiences. In the next six chapters, we will provide tutorials on building four VR solutions. Each project is presented as a series of steps to illustrate the process for completion. However, we want to stress that this is only a start. Use this work as a starting point for your own creativity.

2
Building a Solar System for Google Cardboard

"For the things we have to learn before we can do them, we learn by doing them."

- Aristotle

The process of learning by experience and reflection, better known as *experiential learning*, is central to my teaching philosophy. Throughout this book, we will explore virtual reality development processes by completing projects designed to illustrate the power of VR and the ease of use of the Unity 3D engine. Your role is to use these projects as a starting point for your own work. Complete the projects, reflect on the process, and expand upon them to enrich your learning and creative curiosity.

Our exploration will begin with a visualization of a newly discovered solar system. This project is a dioramic scene, where the user floats in space, observing the movement of planets within the TRAPPIST-1 planetary system. In February 2017, astronomers announced the discovery of seven planets orbiting an ultra-cool dwarf star slightly larger than Jupiter.

We will use this information to build a virtual environment to run on Google Cardboard (Android and iOS) or compatible devices:

Figure 2.1: Artist rendering of the TRAPPIST-1 system

In this chapter, we will cover the following topics:

- **Platform setup**: Download and install platform-specific software needed to build an application on your target device. Experienced mobile developers with the latest Android or iOS SDK may skip this step.
- **Google Cardboard setup**: This package of development tools facilitates display and interaction on a Cardboard device.
- **Unity environment setup**: Initializing Unity's **Project Settings** in preparation for a VR environment.
- **Building the TRAPPIST-1 system**: Design and implement the Solar System project.
- **Build for your device**: Build and install the project onto a mobile device for viewing in Google Cardboard.

Platform setup

Before we begin building the solar system, we must setup our computer environment to build the runtime application for a given VR device. If you have never built a Unity application for Android or iOS, you will need to download and install the **Software Development Kit (SDK)** for your chosen platform. An SDK is a set of tools that will let you build an application for a specific software package, hardware platform, game console, or operating system. Installing the SDK may require additional tools or specific files to complete the process, and the requirements change from year to year, as operating systems and hardware platforms undergo updates and revisions.

To deal with this nightmare, Unity maintains an impressive set of platform-specific instructions to ease the setup process. Their list contains detailed instructions for the following platforms:

- Apple Mac
- Apple TV
- Android
- iOS
- Samsung TV
- Standalone
- Tizen
- Web Player
- WebGL
- Windows

For this project, we will be building for the most common mobile devices: Android or iOS. The first step is to visit either of the following links to prepare your computer:

- **Android**: Android users will need the Android Developer Studio, **Java Virtual Machine (JVM)**, and assorted drivers. Follow this link for installation instructions and files: `https://docs.unity3d.com/Manual/Android-sdksetup.html`.
- **Apple iOS**: iOS builds are created on a Mac and require an Apple Developer account, and the latest version of Xcode development tools. However, if you've previously built an iOS app, these conditions will have already been met by your system. For the complete instructions, follow this link: `https://docs.unity3d.com/Manual/iphone-GettingStarted.html`.

Google Cardboard setup

Like the Unity documentation website, Google also maintains an in-depth guide for the *Google VR SDK for Unity* set of tools and examples. This SDK provides the following features on the device:

- User head tracking
- Side-by-side stereo rendering
- Detection of user interactions (via trigger or controller)
- Automatic stereo configuration for a specific VR viewer
- Distortion correction
- Automatic gyro drift correction

These features are all contained in one easy-to-use package that will be imported into our Unity scene. Download the SDK from the following link, before moving on to the next step: `http://developers.google.com/cardboard/unity/download`.

At the time of writing, the current version of the Google VR SDK for Unity is version 1.110.1 and it is available via a GitHub repository. The previous link should take you to the latest version of the SDK. However, when starting a new project, be sure to compare the SDK version requirements with your installed version of Unity.

Setting up the Unity environment

Like all projects, we will begin by launching Unity and creating a new project. The first steps will create a project folder which contains several files and directories:

1. Launch the Unity application.
2. Choose the **New** option after the application splash screen loads.

3. Create a new project by launching the Unity application. Save the project as `Trappist1` in a location of your choice, as demonstrated in *Figure 2.2*:

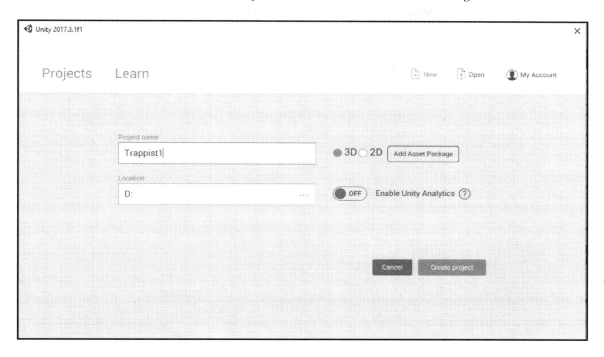

Figure 2.2: New project window

To prepare for VR, we will adjust the **Build Settings** and **Player Settings** windows.

4. Open **Build Settings** from **File | Build Settings**.
5. Select the **Platform** for your target device (iOS or Android).

6. Click the **Switch Platform** button to confirm the change. The Unity icon in the right-hand column of the platform panel indicates the currently selected build platform. By default, it will appear next to the **Standalone** option. After switching, the icon should now be on **Android** or **iOS** platform, as shown in *Figure 2.3*:

Figure 2.3: Build Settings

Note for Android developers: **Ericsson Texture Compression** (**ETC**) is the standard texture compression format on Android. Unity defaults to ETC (default), which is supported on all current Android devices, but it does not support textures that have an alpha channel. ETC2 supports alpha channels and provides improved quality for RBG textures on Android devices that support OpenGL ES 3.0.

Since we will not need alpha channels, we will stick with ETC (default) for this project:

1. Open the **Player Settings** by clicking the button at the bottom of the window. The **PlayerSetting** panel will open in the **Inspector** panel.
2. Scroll down to **Other Settings** (Unity 5.5 thru 2017.1) or **XR Settings** and check the **Virtual Reality Supported** checkbox.
3. A list of choices will appear for selecting VR SDKs. Add Cardboard support to the list, as shown in *Figure 2.4*:

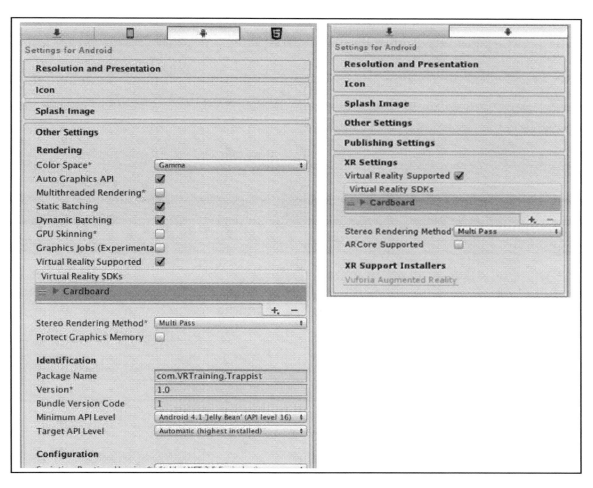

Figure 2.4: Setting the VR SDK in Unity 5.6 or Unity 2017.1+

4. You will also need to create a valid **Bundle Identifier** or **Package Name** under **Identification** section of **Other Settings**. The value should follow the reverse-DNS format of the `com.yourCompanyName.ProjectName` format using alphanumeric characters, periods, and hyphens. The default value must be changed in order to build your application.

Android development note:
Bundle Identifiers are unique. When an app is built and released for Android, the Bundle Identifier becomes the app's package name and cannot be changed. This restriction and other requirements are discussed in this Android documentation link: `http://developer.Android.com/reference/Android/content/pm/PackageInfo.html`.

Apple development note:

Once you have registered a Bundle Identifier to a Personal Team in Xcode, the same Bundle Identifier cannot be registered to another Apple Developer Program team in the future. This means that, while testing your game using a free Apple ID and a Personal Team, you should choose a Bundle Identifier that is for testing only, you will not be able to use the same Bundle Identifier to release the game. An easy way to do this is to add Test to the end of whatever Bundle Identifier you were going to use, for example, `com.MyCompany.VRTrappistTest`. When you release an app, its Bundle Identifier must be unique to your app, and cannot be changed after your app has been submitted to the App Store.

5. Set the **Minimum API Level** to **Android Nougat (API level 24)** and leave the **Target API** on **Automatic**.

6. Close the **Build Settings** window and save the project before continuing.

7. Choose **Assets | Import Package | Custom Package...** to import the `GoogleVRForUnity.unitypackage` previously downloaded from `http://developers.google.com/cardboard/unity/download`. The package will begin decompressing the scripts, assets, and plugins needed to build a Cardboard product.

8. When completed, confirm that all options are selected and choose **Import**.

Once the package has been installed, a new menu titled GoogleVR will be available in the main menu. This provides easy access to the GoogleVR documentation and **Editor Settings**. Additionally, a directory titled GoogleVR will appear in the **Project** panel:

1. Right-click in the **Project** and choose **Create | Folder** to add the following directories: Materials, Scenes, and Scripts.

2. **Choose File | Save Scenes** to save the default scene. I'm using the very original Main Scene and saving it to the Scenes folder created in the previous step.

3. Choose **File | Save Project** from the main menu to complete the setup portion of this project.

Building the TRAPPIST-1 System

Now that we have Unity configured to build for our device, we can begin building our space themes VR environment. We have designed this project to focus on building and deploying a VR experience. If you are moderately familiar with Unity, this project will be very simple. Again, this is by design. However, if you are relatively new, then the basic 3D primitives, a few textures, and a simple orbiting script will be a great way to expand your understanding of the development platform:

1. Create a new script by selecting **Assets | Create | C# Script** from the main menu. By default, the script will be titled NewBehaviourScript. Single click this item in the **Project** window and rename it OrbitController. Finally, we will keep the project organized by dragging OrbitController's icon to the Scripts folder.

2. Double-click the OrbitController script item to edit it. Doing this will open a script editor as a separate application and load the OrbitController script for editing. The following code block illustrates the default script text:

```
using System.Collections;
using System.Collections.Generic;
using UnityEngine;

public class OrbitController : MonoBehaviour {

    // Use this for initialization
    void Start () {

    }

    // Update is called once per frame
```

```
void Update () {

  }
}
```

This script will be used to determine each planet's location, orientation, and relative velocity within the system. The specific dimensions will be added later, but we will start by adding some public variables.

3. Starting on line 7, add the following five statements:

```
public Transform orbitPivot;
public float orbitSpeed;
public float rotationSpeed;
public float planetRadius;
public float distFromStar;
```

Since we will be referring to these variables in the near future, we need a better understanding of how they will be used:

- orbitPivot stores the position of the object that each planet will revolve around (in this case, it is the star TRAPPIST-1).
- orbitalSpeed is used to control how fast each planet revolves around the central star.
- rotationSpeed is how fast an object rotates around its own axis.
- planetRadius represents a planet's radius compared to Earth. This value will be used to set the planet's size in our environment.
- distFromStar is a planet's distance in **Astronomical Units (AU)** from the central star.

4. Continue by adding the following lines of code to the Start() method of the OrbitController script:

```
// Use this for initialization
   void Start () {
// Creates a random position along the orbit path
       Vector2 randomPosition = Random.insideUnitCircle;
       transform.position = new Vector3 (randomPosition.x, 0f,
       randomPosition.y) * distFromStar;

// Sets the size of the GameObject to the Planet radius value
       transform.localScale = Vector3.one * planetRadius;
   }
```

As shown within this script, the `Start()` method is used to set the initial position of each planet. We will add the dimensions when we create the planets, and this script will pull those values to set the starting point of each game object at runtime:

1. Next, modify the `Update()` method by adding two additional lines of code, as indicated in the following code block:

```
// Update is called once per frame. This code block updates the
Planet's position during each
// runtime frame.
    void Update () {
        this.transform.RotateAround (orbitPivot.position,
        Vector3.up, orbitSpeed * Time.deltaTime);
        this.transform.Rotate (Vector3.up, rotationSpeed *
        Time.deltaTime);
    }
```

This method is called once per frame while the program is running. Within `Update()`, the location for each object is determined by computing where the object should be during the next frame. `this.transform.RotateAround` uses the sun's pivot point to determine where the current GameObject (identified in the script by `this`) should appear in this frame. Then `this.transform.Rotate` updates how much the planet has rotated since the last frame.

2. Save the script and return to Unity.

Now that we have our first script, we can begin building the star and its planets. For this process, we will use Unity's primitive 3D GameObject to create the celestial bodies:

1. Create a new sphere using **GameObject | 3D Object | Sphere**. This object will represent the star TRAPPIST-1. It will reside in the center of our solar system and will serve as the pivot for all seven planets.
2. Right-click on the newly created `Sphere` object in the **Hierarchy** window and select **Rename**. Rename the object `Star`.
3. Using the **Inspector** tab, set the object to **Position**: 0,0,0 and **Scale**: 1,1,1.
4. With the Star selected, locate the **Add Component** button in the **Inspector** panel. Click the button and enter `orbitcontroller` in the search box. Double-click on the `OrbitController` script icon when it appears. The script is now a component of the star.
5. Create another sphere using **GameObject | 3D Object | Sphere** and position it anywhere in the scene, with the default scale of 1,1,1. Rename the object `Planet b`.

Figure 2.5, from the TRAPPIST-1 Wikipedia page, shows the relative orbital period, distance from the star, radius, and mass of each planet. We will use these dimensions and names to complete the setup of our VR environment. Each value will be entered as public variables for their associated GameObjects:

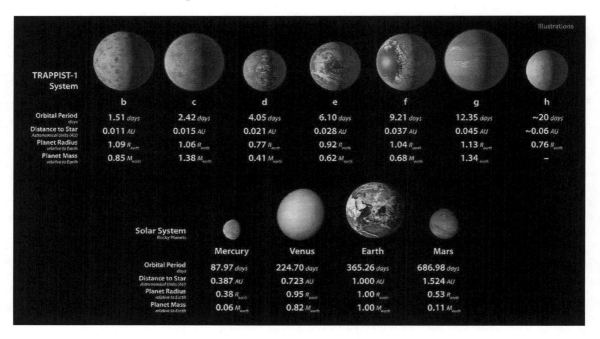

Figure 2.5: TRAPPIST-1 details

6. Apply the `OrbitController` script to the `Planet b` asset by dragging the script icon to the planet in the **Scene** window or the `Planet b` object in the **Hierarchy** window. `Planet b` is our first planet and it will serve as a prototype for the rest of the system.

7. Set the **Orbit Pivot** point of `Planet b` in the **Inspector**. Do this by clicking the Selector Target next to the **Orbit Pivot** field (see *Figure 2.6*). Then, select `Star` from the list of objects. The field value will change from **None (Transform)** to **Star (Transform)**. Our script will use the origin point of the select GameObject as its pivot point.

8. Go back and select the `Star` GameObject and set the **Orbit Pivot** to `Star` as we did with `Planet b`.

9. Save the scene:

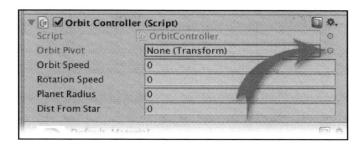

Figure 2.6: Selector Target in the OrbitController script

Now that our template planet has the `OrbitController` script, we can create the remaining planets:

1. Duplicate the `Planet b` GameObject six times, by right-clicking on it and choosing **Duplicate**.
2. Rename each copy `Planet c` through `Planet h`.
3. Set the public variables for each `GameObject`, using the following chart:

GameObject	Orbit Speed	Rotation Speed	Planet Radius	Dist From Star
Star	0	2	6	0
Planet b	.151	5	0.85	11
Planet c	.242	5	1.38	15
Planet d	.405	5	0.41	21
Planet e	.61	5	0.62	28
Planet f	.921	5	0.68	37
Planet g	1.235	5	1.34	45
Planet h	1.80	5	0.76	60

Table 2.1: TRAPPIST-1 gameobject Transform settings

4. Create an empty GameObject by right clicking in the **Hierarchy** panel and selecting **Create Empty**. This item will help keep the **Hierarchy** window organized. Rename the item `Planets` and drag `Planet b`—through `Planet h` into the empty item.

This completes the layout of our solar system, and we can now focus on setting a location for the stationary player. Our player will not have the luxury of motion, so we must determine the optimal point of view for the scene:

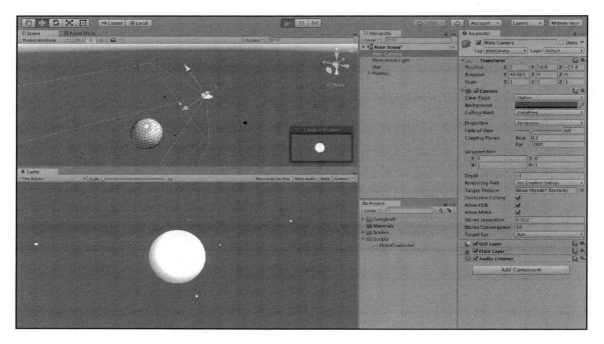

Figure 2.7: Scene and Game windows of the TRAPPIST-1 project

5. Run the simulation.

6. *Figure 2.7* illustrates the layout being used to build and edit the scene. With the scene running and the `Main Camera` selected, use the Move and Rotate tools or the **Transform** fields to readjust the position of the camera in the **Scene** window or to find a position with a wide view of the action in the **Game** window; or a position with an interesting vantage point.

Do not stop the simulation when you identify a position. Stopping the simulation will reset the **Transform** fields back to their original values.

7. Click the small Options gear in the **Transform** panel and select **Copy Component**. This will store a copy of the **Transform** settings to the clipboard:

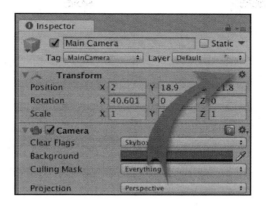

Figure 2.8: Transform Options location

8. Stop the simulation. You will notice that the Main Camera position and rotation have reverted to their original settings. Click the Transform gear again and select **Paste Component Values** to set the **Transform** fields to the desired values.

9. Save the scene and project.

You might have noticed that we cannot really tell how fast the planets are rotating. This is because the planets are simple spheres without details. This can be fixed by adding materials to each planet. Since we really do not know what these planets look like we will take a creative approach and go for aesthetics over scientific accuracy.

The internet is a great source for the images we need. A simple Google search for planetary textures will result in thousands of options. Use a collection of these images to create materials for the planets and the TRAPPIST-1 star:

1. Open a web browser and search Google for `planet textures`. You will need one texture for each planet and one more for the star. Download the textures to your computer and rename them something memorable (that is, `planet_b_mat...`). Alternatively, you can download a complete set of textures from the *Resources* section of the supporting website: `http://zephyr9.pairsite.com/vrblueprints/Trappist1/`.

2. Copy the images to the `Trappist1/Assets/Materials` folder.

3. Switch back to Unity and open the `Materials` folder in the **Project** panel.

4. Drag each texture to its corresponding GameObject in the **Hierarchy** panel. Notice that each time you do this Unity creates a new material and assigns it to the planet GameObject:

Figure 2.9: Scene windows with materials applied to the planet and star

5. Run the simulation again and observe the movement of the planets. Adjust the individual planet **Orbit Speed** and **Rotation Speed** to feel natural. Take a bit of creative license here, leaning more on the scene's aesthetic quality than on scientific accuracy.
6. Save the scene and the project.

For the final design phase, we will add a space themed background using a **Skybox**. Skyboxes are rendered components that create the backdrop for Unity scenes. They illustrate the world beyond the 3D geometry, creating an atmosphere to match the setting.

Skyboxes can be constructed of solids, gradients, or images using a variety of graphic programs and applications. For this project, we will find a suitable component in the **Asset Store**:

1. Load the **Asset Store** from the **Window** menu. Search for a free space-themed skybox using the phrase `space skybox price:0`. Select a package and use the **Download** button to import the package into the **Scene**.
2. Select **Window | Lighting | Settings** from the main menu.

3. In the **Scene** section, click on the Selector Target for the **Skybox Material** and choose the newly downloaded skybox:

Figure 2.10: Game view with the Skybox installed

4. Save the scene and the project.

With that last step complete, we are done with the design and development phase of the project. Next, we will move on to building the application and transferring it to a device.

Building the application

To experience this simulation in VR, we need to have our scene run on a head-mounted display as a stereoscopic display. The app needs to compile the proper viewing parameters, capture and process head tracking data, and correct for visual distortion. When you consider the number of VR devices we would have to account for, the task is nothing short of daunting.

Luckily, Google VR facilitates all of this in one easy-to-use plugin.

The process for building the mobile application will depend on the mobile platform you are targeting. If you have previously built and installed a Unity app on a mobile device, many of these steps will have already been completed, and a few will apply updates to your existing software.

 Note: Unity is a fantastic software platform with a rich community and an attentive development staff. During the writing of this book, we tackled software updates (5.5 through 2017.3) and various changes in the VR development process. Although we are including the simplified building steps, it is important to check Google's VR documentation for the latest software updates and detailed instructions:

Android: https://developers.google.com/vr/unity/get-started

iOS: https://developers.google.com/vr/unity/get-started-ios

Android Instructions

If you are just starting out building applications from Unity, we suggest starting out with the Android process. The workflow for getting your project export from Unity to playing on your device is short and straight forward:

1. On your Android device, navigate to **Settings | About phone or Settings | About Device | Software Info**.
2. Scroll down to Build number and tap the item seven times. A popup will appear, confirming that you are now a developer.
3. Now navigate to **Settings | Developer options | Debugging** and enable **USB debugging**.

Building an Android application

1. In your project directory (at the same level as the `Asset` folder), create a `Build` folder.
2. Connect your Android device to the computer using a USB cable. You may see a prompt asking you to confirm that you wish to enable **USB debugging** on the device. If so, click **OK**.

3. In Unity, select **File** | **Build Settings** to load the Build dialog.

4. Confirm that the **Platform** is set to **Android**. If not choose **Android** and click **Switch Platform**.

5. Note that `Scenes/Main Scene` should be loaded and checked in the **Scenes In Build** portion of the dialog. If not, click the **Add Open Scenes** button to add **Main Scene** to the list of scenes to be included in the build.

6. Click the **Build** button. This will create an Android executable application with the `.apk` file extension.

Invalid command Android error

Some Android users have reported an error relating to the Android SDK Tools location. The problem has been confirmed in many installations prior to Unity 2017.1. If this problem occurs, the best solution is to downgrade to a previous version of the SDK Tools. This can be done by following the steps outlined here:

1. Locate and delete the Android SDK `Tools` folder [Your Android SDK Root]/tools. This location will depend on where the Android SDK package was installed. For example, on my computer the Android SDK Tools folder is found at `C:\Users\cpalmer\AppData\Local\Android\sdk`.

2. Download SDK Tools from `http://dl-ssl.google.com/Android/repository/tools_r25.2.5-windows.zip`.

3. Extract the archive to the SDK root directory.

4. Re-attempt the **Build** project process.

If this is the first time you are creating an Android application, you might get an error indicating that Unity cannot locate your Android SDK root directory. If this is the case, follow these steps:

1. Cancel the build process and close the **Build Settings...** window.

2. Choose **Edit** | **Preferences...** from the main menu.

3. Choose **External Tools** and scroll down to **Android**.

4. Enter the location of your Android SDK root folder. If you have not installed the SDK, click the download button and follow the installation process.

Install the app onto your phone and load the phone into your Cardboard device:

Figure 2.11: Stereoscopic view on an Android device

iOS Instructions

The process for building an iOS app is much more involved than the Android process. There are two different types of builds:

1. Build for testing
2. Build for distribution (which requires an Apple Developer License)

In either case, you will need the following items to build a modern iOS app:

- A Mac computer running OS X 10.11 or later
- The latest version of Xcode
- An iOS device and USB cable
- An Apple ID
- Your Unity project

For this demo, we will build an app for testing and we will assume you have completed the Getting Started steps (`https://docs.unity3d.com/Manual/iphone-GettingStarted.html`) from *Section 1*. If you do not yet have an Apple ID, obtain one from the Apple ID site (`http://appleid.apple.com/`). Once you have obtained an Apple ID, it must be added to Xcode:

1. Open Xcode.
2. From the menu bar at the top of the screen, choose **Xcode | Preferences**. This will open the **Preferences** window.
3. Choose **Accounts** at the top of the window to display information about the Apple IDs that have been added to Xcode.
4. To add an Apple ID, click the plus sign at the bottom left corner and choose **Add Apple ID**.
5. Enter your Apple ID and password in the resulting popup box.
6. Your Apple ID will then appear in the list.
7. Select your Apple ID.
8. Apple Developer Program teams are listed under the heading of Team. If you are using the free Apple ID, you will be assigned to Personal Team. Otherwise, you will be shown the teams you are enrolled in through the Apple Developer Program.

Preparing your Unity project for iOS

1. Within Unity, open the **Build Settings** from the top menu (**File | Build Settings**).
2. Confirm that the **Platform** is set to **iOS**. If not choose **iOS** and click **Switch Platform** at the bottom of the window.
3. Select the **Build & Run** button.

Building an iOS application

1. Xcode will launch with your Unity project.
2. Select your platform and follow the standard process for building an application from Xcode.
3. Install the app onto your phone and load the phone into your Cardboard device.

Summary

Our goal for this book is to provide an experiential learning approach to development. We want to guide your learning, but we will also provide many opportunities to augment your learning with additional creative challenges and links to external sources to expand upon the projects described here.

In this chapter, we looked at the base Unity workflow for developing VR experiences. We provided a stationary solution so that we could focus on the development process. The Cardboard platform provides access to VR content from a mobile platform, but it also allows for touch and gaze controls, which we will explore in the next chapter. Our second activity, an interactive image gallery, will be built for the Samsung VR Gear, but it can also be built for the Google Cardboard platform.

3

Building an Image Gallery System for the Gear VR

"Share your knowledge. It is a way to achieve immortality."
- His Holiness the Dalai Lama

Virtual reality is more than just creating new environments; it can also be used to share real-world experiences with others. Using an array of VR imaging techniques, you can watch a New Orleans street parade, swim with sea turtles in the Great Barrier Reef, ride in a Humvee embedded on Falluja's front lines, or survey the city of Paris from a vantage point high above the Eiffel Tower. With these ideas in mind, our next project will be to build an immersive 360° gallery.

With this project, we will introduce the following concepts:

- User interaction in VR
- Equirectangular images
- The Samsung Gear VR workflow process:

Figure 3.1: Scene and Game window from the VR Gallery project

A virtual image gallery

In this project, we will be creating a stationary VR experience where the user can view images from a photo gallery. It is a simple project with many different applications from travel slideshows to employee orientation to *Where's Waldo* style games. In each use case, the important attribute of the experience is user interaction. By default, the first order of interaction in VR is head movement; the user *controls* the environment through limited, but natural, head gestures. This level of immersion works because these movements allow us to perceive the illusion of reality as the virtual world mimics our expectations of the real world; that is, if you turn your head right, the world pans left. Without this simple interaction, the stereoscopic display cannot trick our brain into perceiving the experience as real.

The Samsung Gear VR platform

For this project, we will use the Samsung Gear VR for the final application. The Gear VR has several advantages over Google Cardboard, most notably a rugged and comfortable form factor, wider field of view, straps for easy fitting, volume controls, and integrated buttons for interaction. It is also powered by Oculus and links to Oculus Home, an interactive desktop and menu system used to browse and launch new and previously purchased applications:

Figure 3.2: Samsung Gear VR with Controller

Process overview – Part 1

Production of the Virtual Reality Gallery will be spread across two chapters. In Part 1, we will focus on constructing the environment and building the project asset. Then, we will move on to Part 2, where the addition of scripts and final polish will make the project ready for a mobile device. The following topics will be discussed here in this chapter:

- Getting started
- Prepping for VR
- Acquiring the Oculus Virtual Reality plugin
- Constructing a panoramic Skybox
- Creating the `Gallery` prefab
- Building the galleries

Getting started in VR

Our first step is to set up our Unity environment. This is a common process for many Unity projects. It entails creating the new project files and adding asset folders for organizing the various elements needed to bring the project to life. Take the following steps to get started:

1. Create a new Unity project called `VRGallery`
2. Create the following folders within the **Project** panel:
   - `Materials`
   - `Prefabs`
   - `Scenes`
   - `Scripts`

3. Save the scene as `WIP_1` and move it into the `Scenes` folder. We will make incremental versions of the scene to aid in debugging. **Work In Progress** (**WIP**).

   Creating an organized folder structure within the `Asset` directory saves lots of time and frustration. This is always the first step when creating a new project. Normally, we would also create a `Texture` directory, but this time we will import sample textures from the resources section of the supporting website:

4. Download the `GalleryImages` package from GitHub Repo for GalleryImages.

This package contains sample images to use in our project. Unity packages are a great way to share assets among projects and developers. One of the things I love about Unity is that project files can be used across multiple platforms. There is no need to create separate files for Windows, Mac and Linux, because the file structure and content is platform agnostic. Just download and open or import into a compatible version of Unity. Take the following steps to import:

1. Choose **Assets | Import Package | Custom Package...** from the main menu and navigate to the `GalleryImages` package.
2. Confirm that everything is selected in the **Unity Import Package** window before clicking the **Import** button. This will create a new `GalleryImages` folder which contains the background and foreground images needed for the project:

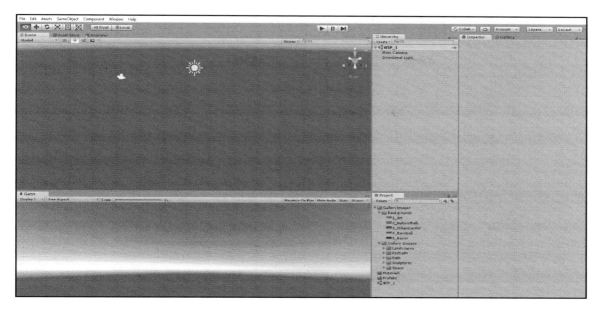

Figure 3.3: Base project file

Prepping for VR

The deliverable for this project will be a VR application for the Samsung Gear VR. To accomplish this, we must change the build settings to accommodate the Android mobile device and load the Oculus Virtual Reality plugin into our scene. The following steps outline this process:

1. Select **Build Settings...** from the **File** menu
2. Select **Android** from the **Platform** list and **ASTC** from the **Texture Compression** dropdown menu
3. Click the **Switch Platform** button to confirm the change
4. Save the scene and project

Acquiring the Oculus SDK package

Unity provides built-in support for most of the virtual reality devices on the market. Additionally, Oculus provides a set of utilities which contains a variety of assets (scripts, prefabs, demonstration scenes, and so on) to facilitate development for the Rift and Samsung Gear VR. Installation of the utilities can be done by importing the Oculus Integration plugin from the **Asset Store** or by downloading the Oculus Utilities for Unity from https://developer.oculus.com/downloads/unity/.

At the time of this writing, the current version of Unity is 2017.2 and the OVRPlugin (included in the Utilities) is 1.18.1. However, as the company is constantly improving the platform, major revisions are always on the horizon. Take the following steps to integrate it:

1. Search for the Oculus Integration plugin in the **Asset Store**
2. Select the package and click the **Import** button

    The Import Unity Package window (see the following screenshot) will display each of the Oculus Utilities assets included in the package.

3. Scroll down about halfway and *uncheck* **Scenes**. These will not be needed for our project. Click the **Import** button at the bottom of the window to continue:

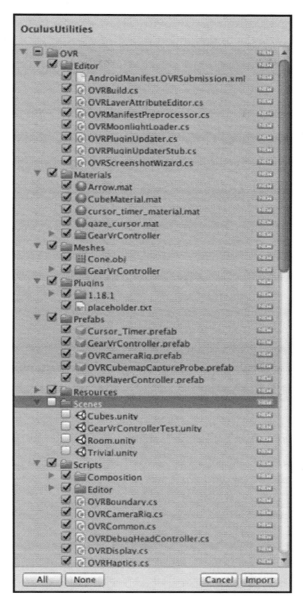

Figure 3.4: Import everything except the Scenes directory

Adding this package will probably require an update of various Oculus scripts. Choose **Go ahead** in the API Update Required dialog to update any obsolete scripts.
If a dialog opens asking to Update Oculus Utilities Plugin, choose **Yes** and restart Unity if asked to do so.

When the import is completed, many new files and directories will be added to the **Project** window. It is important that these files and folders remain where they are. Moving them will result in errors as the location of scripts will be unresolved by the software. Now, take the following steps:

1. Delete the Main Camera GameObject.
2. Browse the **Project** panel to find the OVR/Prefabs directory. Locate the OVRCameraRig prefab and drag it into the **Scene** window.

The OVRPlugin package includes many GameObjects, scripts, and prefabs. These items have been developed to provide content creators with the tools necessary to build new VR experiences. The OVRCameraRig contains multiple cameras and targets to control the VR experience. This camera will serve as the user's viewing portal in our VR environment.

The **Game** window will reveal the scene image as soon as the prefab is added:

1. Set the position of the OVRCameraRig to (0,0,-1.5) in the **Inspector** window
2. Save the Unity scene
3. Use **File** | **Save Scene** to create WIP_2

Constructing a panoramic skybox

By default, Unity Scenes start with a ground plane, horizon line, sky, and Sun. However, these are not individual GameObjects. Instead, it is a panoramic texture mapped to the inside of a cube and we call it a **skybox**. The skybox is drawn in the background behind all other objects and rotates to match the current camera's orientation. When done correctly, the skybox creates an immersive environment within the scene.

Skyboxes are materials created from combining six photographs, each at 90° from each other or by capturing a single 360° **equirectangular panoramic image**. The six-photo method, known as a Cubemap, can be created by shooting images from a single position in each direction; up, right, left, front, back, and down. Equirectangular images are created by capturing or stitching together images into a 3D projection:

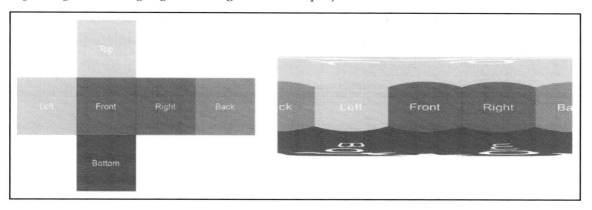

Figure 3.5: Cubemap (left) versus Equirectangular (right) image comparison

An equirectangular panoramic image is a projection where the verticals remain vertical, and the horizon becomes a straight line across the middle of the image. *Figure 3.5* shows how the coordinates in the image relate linearly to pan and tilt angles in the real world. The poles are located at the top and bottom edge and are stretched to the entire width of the image. Areas near the poles are stretched horizontally. In *Figure 3.6*, we can see how this arrangement is applied to a panoramic image:

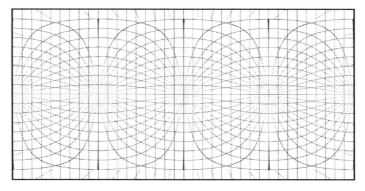

Figure 3.6: Coordinate system in an equirectangular panoramic image

The equirectangular projection is the default output format of many rotating panoramic camera. However, even still images captured via DSLR or smartphone can be edited to meet our needs. One important factor of the capture process is that the images cover a full 360° horizontally and 180° vertically resulting in a final aspect ratio of 2:1. Before applying your own images to this project, be sure the file's height and width values are between 1024x512 and 8192×4096.

The internet is home to hundreds of repositories for viewing and downloading these types of images. We have included a few here for this tutorial, but feel free to create or search for images that fit the theme of your project. For example, Figure 3.7 is the result of a simple Google search on the term *equirectangular images*:

Figure 3.7: Image wrapped to match equirectangular projection

If you are using your own image, it should be imported into the Unity project and stored in the `GalleryImages/Background` folder before continuing:

1. Select an image from `Project/GalleryImages/Backgrounds` directory.

   The `Backgrounds` directory contains sample equirectangular images to be used as backgrounds for our virtual gallery. Feel free to import your own panoramic images to customize the project. When using your own images for the scene background, you need to make sure they fit the 2:1 ratio requirement.

2. Change the **Texture Shape** from **2D** to **Cube** in the **Inspector** panel.
3. Click the **Apply** button to accept the change.
4. Create a new material named `Backdrop` and move it to the `Materials` folder.
5. Change the **Shader** for **Backdrop** from **Standard** to **Skybox | Cubemap**:

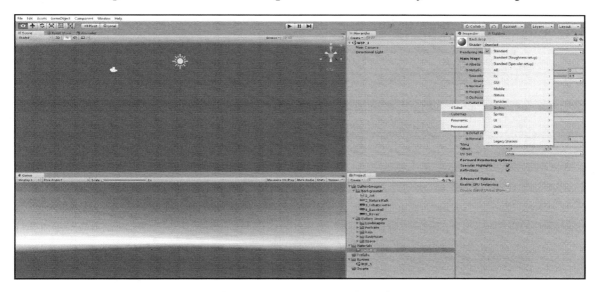

Figure 3.8: Setting the shader for the new material to Skybox | Cubemap

6. With the material still selected, click the **Select** button inside of the `Cubemap` icon preview. Select **Backdrop** from the selection box to set the skybox.

With the new skybox created, we can now assign it to the scene:

1. Choose **Window | Lightning | Settings** to open the **Lighting** panel.
2. Click the **Skybox Material** selection target to access the scene's skyboxes.
3. Double-click **Backdrop** to apply our skybox to the scene.

The **Backdrop** skybox is now displayed in both the **Scene** and **Game** windows. Right-click and drag around the **Scene** window to preview our environment. With the skybox in place, we can now move on to creating a VR camera:

1. Save your scene and Unity project.
2. Use **File | Save Scene** to create `WIP_3`:

Figure 3.9: 1_Art image used as a skybox

Creating the Gallery prefab

When it runs, our project will house multiple images in individual *galleries*. Each gallery will be a self-contained prefab containing thumbnail previews, scripts for user interaction, and a category title. The next several steps will involve building the first gallery. Once completed, these objects will become prefabs for creating additional image galleries with their own unique content:

1. Make an empty GameObject and title it `GalleryHolder`.
   This object is the primary receptacle for the individual galleries. All images and canvases will exist inside of this container.
2. Move `GalleryHolder` to (0,0,0).

3. Add a **Canvas** to the `GalleryHolder` GameObject and name it `Gallery`. Do this by right-clicking on `GalleryHolder` in the **Hierarchy** window and choosing **UI | Canvas**.

4. Rename the Canvas GameObject `Gallery` in the **Inspector**.

   This canvas will be the parent of the individual UI elements for a single gallery. Everything we need to build and display to the user will be included here. This will serve as the first category of images and later we will duplicate it to create additional galleries. *Figure 3.9* is a sketch of the gallery layout we are building. The final gallery will have a large image area with five smaller thumbnails:

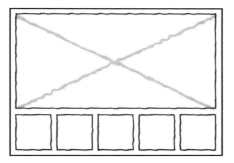

Figure 3.10: Layout sketch of the gallery GameObjects

   Creating the new canvas will also create an `EventSystem` in the **Hierarchy** panel. We will not need to modify or adjust the object. Its purpose is to manage the processing and handling of events within the scene. It works in conjunction with several modules and must be present.

5. Set the **Canvas Render Mode** to **World Space**: Select the `Gallery` element and find the Canvas component in the **Inspector** panel. Change the **Render Mode** to **World Space**.

Render Mode controls how canvases are displayed in Unity scenes. There are three options:

- **Screen Space – Overlay**: Overlay is the default value. In this mode, the canvas is drawn directly on top of the scene. This is helpful when creating a UI that must conform or resize to changes in the resolution or scale of the scene.

- **Screen Space – Camera**: As in Overlay, in this mode objects are drawn on top of the scene, but here the canvas can be set at a specific distance from the camera. This means that besides being affected by the scale and resolution of the scene's camera, the UI elements are also affected by the perspective and distortion created by manipulating the camera's field of view and frustum.
- **World Space**: Here the canvas will behave as any other element in our scene and can be incorporated into the world. The size can be set manually instead of being tied to the camera and scene. It is important to use it here because we want the UI elements to be fixed in space, so that as the user's perspective changes with normal head movement, the UI elements will be anchored to a specific position.

6. With the `Gallery` canvas selected, choose the Event Camera target selector in the Canvas component. Double-click `CenterEyeAnchor` from the Select Camera list to set the value. *Figure 3.11* shows the **Canvas** and **Canvas Scaler (Script)** components of the `Gallery` GameObject:

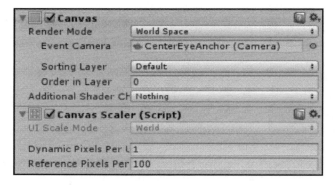

Figure 3.11: Canvas component for the Gallery GameObject

The `CenterEyeAnchor` GameObject is a prefab within the `OVRCameraRig`. It coincides with the center position between the left and right camera, which are used to create simulated vision.

7. Set the position, size (height and width), pivot, rotation, and scale transformations to the values indicated in *Figure 3.13*:

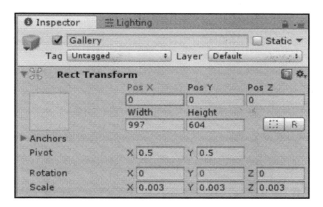

Figure 3.12: Rect Transform settings for the Gallery GameObject

By default, the `Canvas` object will be scaled to cover the camera's entire field of view. To fit the object within the player's vision, the `Gallery` GameObject must be scaled down. In this example we used `0.003` to allow three galleries to fit in the space. Your project might need a different scale based on the number of Canvases needed and their distance from the `OVRCameraRig`.

8. Save the scene and Unity project.

You will note that our `Gallery` object is nearly invisible in the **Game** window. This is because our `Gallery` object is a container for the UI elements we will need to present to the user. Without images or text, the object is only visible in the **Scene** window as a rectangle with a thin white stroke. After the optional font installation in the next step we will create UI elements to be dynamically updated and controlled by scripts.

Optional custom fonts

Before creating the new GameObjects, we should address an optional asset that might be needed. If specific fonts have been identified for this project, those fonts must be added to the project as new assets. If the font assets are not added, the final `.apk` file will display a default font determined by the mobile device. This will alter the typography of your concept:

1. [Option] In the **Project** window, add a new folder called `Fonts`.
2. [Option] Import your chosen `TrueType` or `OpenType` font file (`.ttf` or `.otf`) into the newly created `Fonts` folder.

Building the galleries

We are now ready to build our galleries. To do so, take the following steps:

1. Select the `Gallery` GameObject and add a child object by right-clicking and choosing **UI | Text**.
   This will create a new text object within our `Gallery` object. Adjust the text object's attributes as follows:
   - Rename the object `CategoryTitle`.
   - Set the Y position to `252` in the Rect Transform component.
   - Replace the `New Text` text in the **Text (Script)** component to `Category Title`. It should be noted that this text is a placeholder and the actual title will be set using a script.
   - In the **Character** section, choose a **Font** and **Font Style** to your liking.
   - Set the **Horizontal** and **Vertical Overflow** to **Overflow** under **Paragraph**. The **Default** value, **Wrap**, will attempt to display the category name within the **Text** space. Changing this value now will make it easier to determine the necessary font size.
   - Set the **Font Size** to `60` or a size appropriate for your text.

 If the **Horizontal Overflow** and **Vertical Overflow** values are set to **Wrap** when choosing a font size, the text will momentarily vanish. This is because the resized text is larger than the text field which will truncate the content.

A good strategy for determining the correct font size is to enter the longest text string into each of the **Text (Script)** fields. This method will make it easier to judge the line lengths and negative space between the canvases. You will probably need to adjust this value a few times, but starting with this strategy should help find the correct size:

- Set the **Paragraph Alignment** to Center and Middle.
- Finally set a color, which works for your scene. In this example, we are setting the category title to 60-point ClearSans-Bold, with a normal style and white color.

Creating the image display element (FullImage)

It is now time to create the image display element. Take the following steps to do so:

1. Reselect the `Gallery` GameObject.
2. Add another child object by right-clicking and choosing **UI | Image**. This will create a new 100 x 100 pixel, blank image object within our `Gallery` object. Since we have not identified a source, the object will appear as a white rectangle in the middle of the `Gallery`. Adjust the image object's attributes as follows:
   - Rename the object `FullImage`
   - Set the following; Y position = 30, **Width** = 604 and **Height** = 340

Now that we have a container for the primary image, we will begin building a container for the preview images. When the application is running, these thumbnails will provide the user with a target for selecting the next image to view. Each preview slot will be filled with a 2D Sprite that will be used to swap the currently displayed `FullImage` image. A set of sample images have been included in the `Project | Gallery` Images directory to continue following along with this process. However, if you're feeling creative, import your own images and continue with those:

1. Create another empty GameObject in the `Gallery` canvas and rename it `PreviewHolder`.
2. Set the position to (0, -220, 0).
3. Add alignment components.
   To make the `Gallery` prefab as versatile as possible we need to be prepared for images of varying sizes. We will do this by using two of Unity's built in script components. Add the following components to the `PreviewHolder` GameObject by selecting the `PreviewHolder` and clicking the **Add Component** button in the **Inspector** panel:
   - **Horizontal Layout Group (Script)**: The Horizontal Layout Group component creates a structured layout for a series of child elements. The elements are put in a horizontal grid based on the scripts attributes. Use the following values to setup the script for our galleries:
     - **Spacing**: 25
     - **Child Alignment**: Middle Center
     - Confirm that both **Width** and **Height** are *checked* for the **Child Force Expand**

- **Content Size Fitter (Script)**: Like the Horizontal Layout Group, the Content Size Fitter is used to organize the placement and layout of the preview thumbnails. In this case, the component helps determine how the child objects will fit within the `PreviewHolder`. Use the following values to arrange the thumbnail previews:
  - **Horizontal Fit**: Preferred Size
  - **Vertical Fit**: Preferred Size:

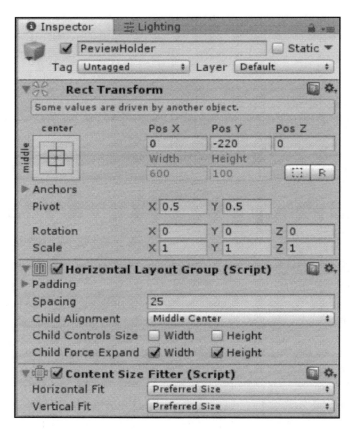

Figure 3.13: PreviewHolder Rect Transform and components

It should be noted that, because we are using **Horizontal Layout Group (Script)** and **Content Size Fitter (Script)**, the `PreviewHolder` does not need a size. Its size will grow based on the number of child elements attached to the GameObject. Additionally, the child objects will be properly aligned to the center and middle of the `PreviewHolder`.

4. Create image thumbnail containers:
    - Like the `FullImage` object, each thumbnail will be a UI Image. Right-click the `PreviewHolder` and choose **UI | Image** to create a blank thumbnail. This will be our first thumbnail, rename it `Preview (1)`.

5. Add a blank script to the `Preview (1)` GameObject called `ImageSelector`:
    - Each thumbnail will be clickable by our user. We will look at the actual scripts in the next chapter, but for now, we will add a blank script to the **Preview** thumbnail before it is duplicated. Select the `Preview (1)`. GameObject and click **Add Component** in the **Inspector** window. Choose **New Script** from the pop-up menu. Name the script `ImageSelector` and make sure its language is **C Sharp**. Finally choose the **Create and Add** button to finish this step:

Figure 3.14: Create a new script

6. Move the `ImageSelector` script into the `Scripts` folder.

7. Duplicate the `Preview (1)` GameObject four more times to create five thumbnail GameObjects:

Figure 3.15: GalleryHolder with one Gallery

Creating a controller and a scene controller script

The last object we need to create is a scene controller with an attached `SceneController` script. A `Controller` GameObject is often used as a repository for scripts that need to run but are not attached to any object. These scripts generally *listen* for specific actions (like those from a player) and manage multiple instances (like those generated by AI GameObjects) within a scene:

1. Create an empty GameObject in the **Hierarchy** window and rename it `Controller`.

2. Add a blank script to the `Controller` called `SceneController`. This will be our last script and like the `ImageSelector` we will modify it in the next chapter.

3. Move the `SceneController` scripts into the `Script` folder.
4. Save the scene and Unity project.
5. Use **File** | **Save Scene** to create `WIP_4`.

We now have a completed `Gallery` GameObject. From this, we will build more galleries to hold additional titles, images, and thumbnails.

Creating a gallery prefab

With the `Gallery` GameObject's structure completed, we can build out the scene by creating additional galleries. Instead of simply copying and pasting to create new objects, we will convert the initial `Gallery` GameObject into a prefab. Unity prefabs are GameObject templates that retain the same components and properties as the original object(s). With the traditional copy and paste method, each additional copy is an independent object with no reference to the original. However, prefab GameObjects are instances of the original prefab asset(s) and as such, editing the prefab asset will update prefab instances in the scene.

Prefabs are denoted in the **Hierarchy** window by blue text and by having a cube-like icon in the **Project** window:

1. Select the `Gallery` GameObject and drag it into the `Prefabs` folder in the **Project** window. This will create an asset with the same name. *Figure 3.18* illustrates the process of creating the prefab:

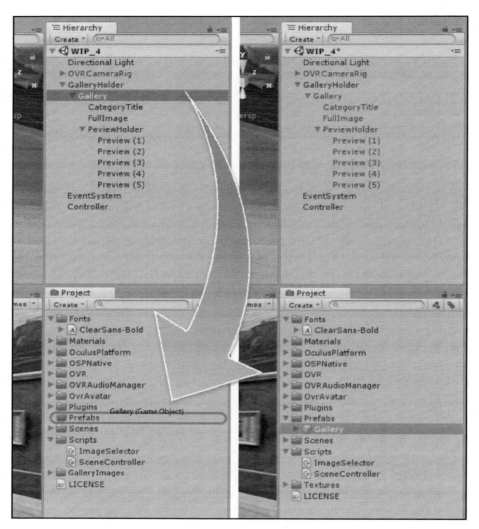

Figure 3.16: Scene with completed Gallery prefab. Note that the blue items are prefabs

2. Create additional galleries. Now that we have a prefab, we can use it to create additional `Gallery` GameObjects in the scene. Each new gallery will have the same properties, settings, and components as our original `Gallery` GameObject. Drag two more `Gallery` prefabs into the `GalleryHolder` GameObject.

3. Rename the prefabs to match your content. For our example we gave them unique names with the `Gallery -` prefix:

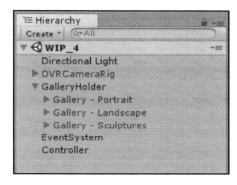

Figure 3.17: Renamed gallery prefabs

4. Use the **Inspector** panel to set the X positions to the following values:

GameObject	Pos X
Gallery - Portraits	-4
Gallery - Landscapes	0
Gallery - Sculptures	-4

This will line up the new galleries horizontally within the scene. Feel free to adjust the values to meet the needs of your project.

5. Save the scene and Unity project.

6. Use `File | Save Scene` as to create `WIP_5`.

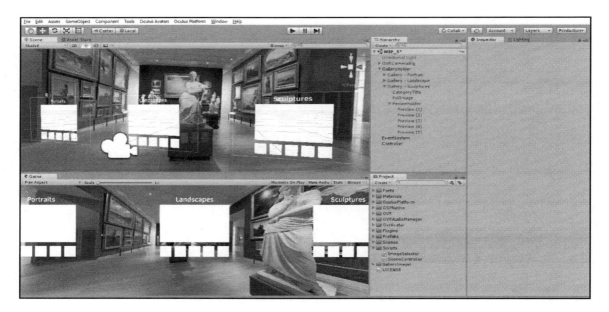

Figure 3.18: Completed environment

Summary

This completes the first half of the project. In this chapter we have constructed the Unity environment. The scene we have created can be customized with additional galleries, alternative backgrounds, or varied gallery layouts. In the next chapter, we will expand the scene by adding images to the galleries, creating scripts to handle user interactions, engaging in the testing process and finalizing the project for deployment on a mobile device.

4

Adding User Interactions to the Virtual Gallery Project

"Learning is not attained by chance, it must be sought for with ardor and diligence."

- Abigail Adams

In this chapter, we will expand on the virtual gallery environment by adding scripts to control user interactions and building, the final executable. The steps outlined here are for the novice programmer, but our hope is that anyone with C# experience will expand these lessons to create something new and innovative:

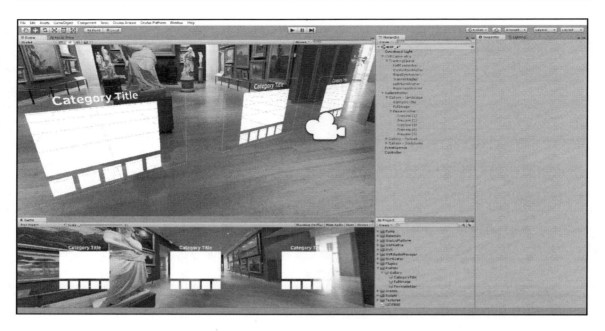

Figure 4.1: Virtual Gallery environment in the Unity engine

Our Virtual Gallery project is coming along nicely. To complete it, we only need to define the scripts, add images, and build an executable for the Gear VR. However, before we get started on the scripts, we need to discuss how virtual interaction works. The following list outlines the phases for finalizing the project:

- Facilitating user interaction
- Using Raycasters and the `StandaloneInput` module for user interaction
- Building the `ImageSelector` and `SceneController` scripts
- Image collection, preparation, and inclusion
- Building an executable

Facilitating user interaction

Unity provides various components for facilitating user input. These components are used first to identify if the user is looking at a specific GameObject, if the user has interacted with a touch device, and how a GameObject should respond to input from a touch device. Let's take a brief look at the components we need for this project.

Raycasters

When we created the first Canvas for the scene, Unity also added an item called `EventSystem`. An `EventSystem` is used to detect where current input events need to be sent and Raycasters provide that information. Think of a Raycaster as a visible laser pointer. When evoked in your scene, the Raycaster sends out a ray which reports the object or objects it has collided with. For our project, we will be using a Graphic Raycaster, but there are also two other types of Raycasters to consider:

- **Graphic Raycaster**: Queries all UI elements in a canvas to determine if any item collides with the ray. This type also has a few properties which determine the conditions in which objects can be ignored.
- **Physics 2D Raycaster**: Can identify 2D physics elements.
- **Physics Raycaster**: For 3D physics elements.

StandaloneInput module

If you have used previous versions of Unity, you may have used the Touch Input module to determine if a touch device was being activated (single press, continuous press, double-pressed, or released). As of Unity 5.6, the Touch Input module has been depreciated and replaced with the `StandaloneInput` module. The module works with touch devices by sending a pointer event for touching or swiping in response to a user input. It uses the scene's Raycasters to calculate which elements are being touched.

These items will be used to determine when the user is looking at an image or collection and what to do when the user taps or swipes the Gear VR trackpad.

Now that we have a better understanding of this tool, we can move on to the project's first script.

Image selector

The `ImageSelector` script will use `GetMouseButtonDown` and a Graphic Raycaster to determine if the user has selected one of the `Preview` GameObjects. If these two events are simultaneously true, then the image associated with the `Preview` GameObject will be assigned to the `FullImage` GameObject. In the following steps, we'll create the `ImageSelector` script, which will then be applied to the `Preview` GameObjects:

1. Double-click the `ImageSelector` script in the `Project/Scripts` directory to open it in the default editor.

2. The first step is to let Unity know what components are going to be used in the script. Since we'll be checking to see if the Raycaster collides with a UI element, we'll need the `UnityEngine.UI` and `UnityEngine.EventSystems` components. Likewise, line 8 calls up the Graphic Raycaster, which is how we'll be interacting with the **Preview** thumbnails.

3. Modify the `Start()` and `Update()` methods, as indicated in the following script:

   ```
   using System.Collections;
   using System.Collections.Generic;
   using UnityEngine;
   using UnityEngine.UI;
   using UnityEngine.EventSystems;

   [RequireComponent(typeof(GraphicRaycaster))]

   public class ImageSelector : MonoBehaviour {

   // Use this for initialization
   void Start () {
   }

   // Update is called once per frame
   void Update () {

   }
   }
   ```

4. We'll need the following public variables to present unique content for each gallery image. Add the following public variables before the `Start()` method:

   ```
   public string categoryTitleName;
   public Text categoryTitle;
   public Image fullImage;
   public Material hilightMaterial;
   ```

```
private void Start () {

}
```

Next, we'll modify the `Start()` and `Update()` functions. These blocks of code will control what happens when the GameObject appears in the scene and how it should respond while the scene is running.

5. Modify the `Start()` and `Update()` methods, as indicated in the following script:

```
private void Start () {
        categoryTitle.text = categoryTitleName;
}

private void Update () {
        if (Input.GetMouseButtonDown(0)) {
        OnPointerDown ();
    }
}
```

 The `OnPointerDown` function will appear read, because it has not been defined.

In the `Start()` method, the `categoryTitle.text` code is used to replace the `Category Title` default text with the value attached to the GameObject having this script. We will see this in action once the script has been completed and the values have been set for the `Preview` GameObjects.

The if statement in the `Update` method checks to see if the user has pressed a button on a controller or touch device. In our case, `GetMouseButtonDown(0)` refers to the Gear VR's trackpad button and, if it has been pressed, the `OnPointerDown()` function will be called.

Setting touch control

Accepting user input will be done as part of a two-step process when the Gear VR's trackpad button is pressed. First, we need to determine if the user clicked on a `selectable` GameObject: if this is TRUE, we then need to capture which GameObject was selected and, finally we need to switch the `FullImage` with the image of the current GameObject. We'll address identifying and capturing the GameObject (our Preview images) within the `OnPointerDown` function.

As mentioned at the start of this chapter, we will use a Graphic Raycaster to project a ray into the scene. However, instead of doing this all the time, we only need to do this when the trackpad button has been pressed. We can then determine if the ray collides with a UI GameObject and, in the event that it does collide, we can store the required GameObject attributes. Use the following link for a detailed explanation of the `PointerEventData` in Unity's documentation. It contains a complete list of attributes captured by this data type: `https://docs.unity3d.com/ScriptReference/EventSystems.PointerEventData.html`:

1. Add the following code after the `Update()` method:

```
public void OnPointerDown () {
    GraphicRaycaster gr = GetComponent<GraphicRaycaster> ();
    PointerEventData data = new PointerEventData (null);
    data.position = Input.mousePosition;

    List<RaycastResult> results =new List<RaycastResult> ();
    gr.Raycast (data, results);

    if (results.Count > 0) {
        OnPreviewClick (results [0].gameObject);
        }
    }
```

 The `OnPreviewClick` function will appear read because it has not been defined.

When the Gear VR's trackpad button is pressed, we create a `GraphicRaycaster` called `gr`, a variable called data to store the current `mousePosition` and an empty list for the collided GameObjects called results. So, when the button is pressed a ray, `gr`, is created which starts at the camera's location and points through the click location. All game objects which collide with the ray are then stored in the result list. For our gallery, we only need the topmost GameObject, which will have an index of `0`. We then pass this object along to a new function which will handle switching the `Preview` image with the `FullImage` image.

2. Add the following code after the `OnPointerDown()` method:

```
void OnPreviewClick (gameObject thisButton) {
    Image previewImage = thisButton.GetComponent<Image> ();
    if (previewImage != null) {
    fullImage.sprite = previewImage.sprite;
    fullImage.type = Image.Type.Simple;
    fullImage.preserveAspect = true;
```

```
    }
  }
```

The `OnPointerDown()` method determines which **Preview** thumbnail was being selected and it does so by casting a ray from the main camera to the `mouseclick` location. Now that we know which **Preview** was chosen, we'll create the `OnPreviewClick` (another custom function) which will set the `FullImage` sprite to be the same as the selected **Preview** sprite.

The function works by passing along a GameObject when called from `OnPointerDown`. In `OnPreviewClick()` the GameObject is stored locally as the variable `thisButton` and its image component is copied to the variable `previewImage`.

Now that we have the image to swap, we check to make sure the image is not empty by testing for a null value with an if statement. As long as the value is not null, we can set `fullImage.sprite` to the same image as `previewImage.sprite`. The next two commands are used to make sure the image displays properly on the new GameObject.

Creating feedback for the user

When developing any type of user interface, it's important to provide a system to help guide the experience. In a virtual setting, this is even more important if the user's input method is a Gaze Input.

Without direct input (like a mouse and cursor), we need to create an indirect method which is just as effective. For this project, we'll use a visual glow to indicate when a `selectable` object is being gazed upon by the user. In the following code snippet, `OnPointerEnter` and `OnPointerExit` functions, provided by the `EventSystem`, will be our feedback mechanism. With these functions, we will add a highlight material and stroke to the `selectable` GameObject:

1. Add the following functions after `OnPreviewClick()`:

```
public void OnPointerEnter (Image image) {
    // when the user's gaze points to image, this statement
highlights the gameObject
    image.material = hilightMaterial;
}

public void OnPointerExit (Image image) {
    image.material = null;
}
```

When the pointer (an invisible object directed by the user's gaze) enters the Preview GameObject, OnPointerEnter changes the object's material to hilightMaterial which will be a highlight material set as a public variable. When the pointer leaves the GameObject, the material will be set to *none* to indicate that the object is no longer clickable.

2. Save the script.
3. Validate the changes.
4. Switch back to Unity, select any preview thumbnail GameObject (that is, Gallery | PreviewHolder | Preview (2)) and note that the Image Selector component in the **Inspector** window now has four additional value fields; **Category Title Name**, **Category Title**, **Full Image**, and **Hilight Material**:

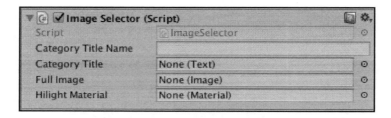

Figure 4.2: Public variables in the Image Selector component of a Preview GameObject

Scene controller

As was originally stated, this project lets a user select images from multiple image galleries. So far, we've learned how to create the virtual environment, created canvases to hold gallery images, and created a script for facilitating the user's ability to select images from preview thumbnails. Next, we need a tool for navigating through multiple galleries. This SceneController script will read the user's swiping direction to determine which gallery to display next. Instead of going into deep details on every line, we'll focus on the functions and commands which are related to the Gear VR's trackpad and moving in VR space:

1. Double-click the SceneController script in the Project/Scripts directory to open the base script in your default editor.

2. Add variables and revise the `Start()` method as shown here:

```
using System.Collections;
using System.Collections.Generic;
using UnityEngine;

public class SceneController : MonoBehaviour {
public gameObject galleryHolder;
public float slideSpeed;
private OVRTouchpad.TouchArgs touchArgs;
private OVRTouchpad.TouchEvent touchEvent;
private bool isMoving;

void Start () {
    OVRTouchpad.Create ();
    OVRTouchpad.TouchHandler += SwipeHandler;
}
```

The `SceneController` script will require a mix of five public and private variables. The first variable, `galleryHolder`, identifies the GameObject that holds our galleries. In our project, the aptly named `Gallery Holder` serves this purpose. This script will use the user's swipe motion to cycle through the individual galleries. The variables `slideSpeed` and `isMoving` take care of the swipe velocity and prevent the galleries from moving too far too quickly.

The last variables to address are associated with the `OVRTouchpad` which is an interface to the `touchpad` class. These variables, `touchArgs` and `touchEvent`, help determine the type of touch created when the user interacts with the trackpad.

3. Modify the `Update()` loop to match the following script:

```
void Update () {
    #if UNITY_EDITOR
    if (!isMoving) {
      if (Input.GetKeyDown (KeyCode.RightArrow)) {
        StartCoroutine (SwipeRight
(galleryHolder.transform.position.x));
        } else if (Input.GetKeyDown (KeyCode.LeftArrow)) {
        StartCoroutine (SwipeLeft
(galleryHolder.transform.position.x));
      }
    }
    #endif
  }
```

The update loop runs about 60 times per second while the scene is playing. On each loop, we need first to determine if the trackpad has been touched, and then perform an action based on that interaction. While testing the application in Unity, we don't have access to the Gear's trackpad. Luckily, Unity provides a **Platform Dependent Compilation (PDC)** feature which will help us with this problem.

The code between the `#if UNITY_EDITOR` and `#endif` statements will only run within the Unity Editor and will not be complied within our final application build. This lets us simulate a user device swipe by pressing the left or right arrow while still in Unity. Without this work-around, we would have to build and install the application on the Gear VR device to see the intended results.

 Learn more about the PDC in the Unity documentation.
https://docs.unity3d.com/Manual/PlatformDependentCompilation.html.

The code between `#if` and `#endif` checks to see if the left or right arrow has been clicked and, if so, we call the `SwipeRight` or `SwipeLeft` functions which we'll design next. However, this only happens if `Gallery Holder` is not moving, as indicated by the if (`!isMoving`) statement. This condition is needed to prevent a double-swipe on the GameObject.

4. Add the `SwipeHandler()` function after the `Update()` method:

```
void SwipeHandler (object sender, System.EventArgs e) {
    touchArgs = (OVRTouchpad.TouchArgs) e;
    touchEvent = touchArgs.TouchType;

    if (!isMoving) {
      if (touchEvent == OVRTouchpad.TouchEvent.Left) {
        StartCoroutine (SwipeLeft
        (galleryHolder.transform.position.x));
      }
      else if (touchEvent == OVRTouchpad.TouchEvent.Right) {
         StartCoroutine (SwipeRight
         (galleryHolder.transform.position.x));
      }
    }
}
```

5. Complete the `SceneController` script by adding the `SwipeRight` and `SwipeLeft` functions after `SwipeHandler()`:

```
private IEnumerator SwipeRight (float startingXPos) {
    while (galleryHolder.transform.position.x != startingXPos - 4)
{
        isMoving = true;
        galleryHolder.transform.position =
        Vector3.MoveTowards (galleryHolder.transform.position, new
        Vector3 (startingXPos - 4,
galleryHolder.transform.position.y,
        0f), slideSpeed * Time.deltaTime);
        yield return null;
    }
    isMoving = false;
  }

private IEnumerator SwipeLeft (float startingXPos) {
    while (galleryHolder.transform.position.x != startingXPos + 4)
{
        isMoving = true;
        galleryHolder.transform.position = Vector3.MoveTowards
        (galleryHolder.transform.position,
        new Vector3 (startingXPos + 4,
        galleryHolder.transform.position.y, 0f),
        slideSpeed * Time.deltaTime);
        yield return null;
    }
    isMoving = false;
  }
```

The `SwipeHandler()` function mimics the `#if UNITY_EDITOR` by accepting inputs when the `Gallery Holder` is not moving. Then the `SwipeRight()` and `SwipeLeft()` functions move the `Gallery Holder` GameObject four units left or right from its starting position at a speed we'll set after applying the script.

6. Save the script.
7. Return to Unity and add the script to the `Controller` GameObject.
8. With the `Controller` GameObject selected, drag the `GalleryHolder` GameObject from the **Hierarchy** window to the `GalleryHolder` field of the **Scene Controller (Script)** component.

9. Set the **Slide Speed** to 5.
   This will be a default value. Feel free to change the value after the script has been properly tested.
10. Save the script and the project before proceeding.

With the scripts in place, our project is almost complete. The next steps are to add and apply imagery to the UI Image elements, `link` GameObject scripts to the correct targets, and build the Gear VR application.

Image collection

Before moving to the the next step, you'll want to make sure you have the gallery images imported into Unity.

Our project is themed as an art gallery, and because of this we are dedicating individual gallery prefabs to portraits, landscapes, and sculptures. However, you are free to use whatever theme makes sense for your project. We envisioned this template being used to craft employee-training tools, college virtual tours, cultural site visits, and professional development applications. So, use your imagination and stretch the project to meet your needs.

Because we chose an art gallery, we used Google to collect common images to match the theme. Once you have collected your images, move on to the next step.

Adding imagery

To complete this phase of the project, we'll need to assign your collected images to the blank UI Image objects we used as placeholders. This is not a difficult process, but it does require one additional step which might not be obvious to new Unity users. Instead of applying standard imported image assets directly to the placeholders, we need to convert the image assets to sprites.

The process is outlined as followed:

1. Right-click on `Gallery Images` in the **Project** window and choose **Create |
   Folder**.
2. Rename the folder to match your gallery content.
   In our example, we created folders for `Landscapes`, `Portraits`, and
   `Sculptures` as shown in the following image:

Figure 4.3: New folders to contain gallery images

3. Import images into the new folders. This can be done within Unity by right-
   clicking on a folder and choosing **Import New Asset...** or by navigating to the
   folder from your computer's desktop and copying the files there. Once imported,
   these images are now Unity Textures.

4. Change the image **Texture Type** from **Default** to **Sprite (2D and UI)**. Textures are image files applied to GameObjects. The initial value provides the most common properties for applying images in a 3D environment. By default, we can apply them to 3D objects, but they will not work for our UI elements. So, select each gallery image and change the **Texture Type** to **Sprite (2D and UI)**, as indicated in *Figure 4.4*. Click the **Apply** button to confirm the change:

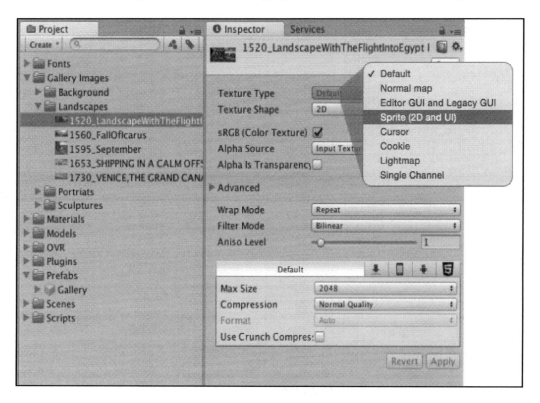

Figure 4.4: Changing the Texture Type of the 1520 landscape image from Default to Sprite (2D and UI)

Note: To convert multiple images, select each image by shift-clicking before changing the Default value in the **Inspector** window. Click the **Apply** button to commit the change.

When this is completed, you'll note that the converted asset changes from a single entry to a nested item with a sprite component.

5. Select a `PreviewHolder | Preview (x)` GameObject in the **Hierarchy** and assign a source to its **Image (Script)** component.
This can be done by using the Target Selector or dragging the correct image to the **Source Image** field. *Figure 4.5* shows the dragging method, which I believe is the easiest way to assign the image source:

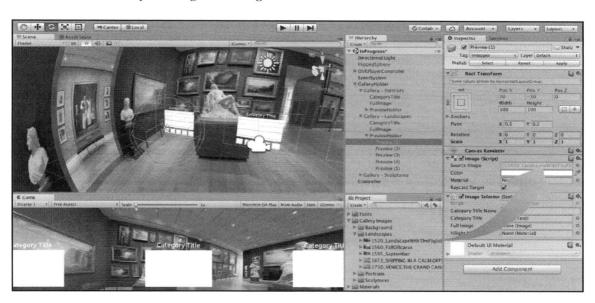

Figure 4.5: Assigning an Image Source to a Preview (1) GameObject using the drag and drop method

6. Repeat this process for the `Preview (x)` images in each of the galleries. Complete these steps for the remaining `Preview` thumbnails in each gallery.

As an optional step, consider clicking the **Preserve Aspect** checkbox in each **Image (Script)** component. Choosing this option will scale the thumbnail image to fill the space. *Figure 4.6* illustrates how this option affects the row of preview images:

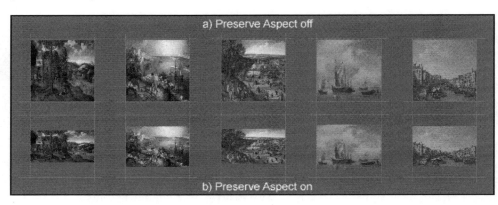

Figure 4.6: Comparison of Preserve Aspect option for Preview (x) GameObjects

Use a highlight material as feedback

When creating the `ImageSelector` script, we discussed the importance of creating a feedback mechanism to help the user determine which object is being viewed. In the script, we created a public variable called `hilightMaterial` but, at that time, we had not defined a material to be used. The following steps outline the creation process:

1. Choose **Create | Material** in the **Project** window menu.
2. Rename the material `Highlight`.
3. Choose a color with high contrast as your highlight. A high-contrast color makes it easier to tell which object is being gazed upon. If you background image is dark, select something very bright and vice versa. I prefer colors in the bright-orange spectrum because they often pop on light or dark backgrounds.

Assigning values

With the preview images in place, we can finish setting the remaining GameObject values. For this process, it is helpful to select all of the `Preview` images in a single `Gallery`. When selected using this method, we can apply multiple values at one time. Follow the steps below to set the public variables for the `Preview` images. All values should be set in the **Inspector** window:

1. Select `Preview (1)` thru `Preview (5)` in the first `Gallery`. Selection can be verified by viewing the highlighted elements in the **Hierarchy** window and preview space at the bottom of the **Inspector** window.
2. Enter a name for this collection of images in the **Category Title Name** field in the **Image Selector (Script)** component in the **Inspector** window.
3. Drag the `Gallery`'s `CategoryTitle` GameObject from the **Hierarchy** window to the **Category Title** field.
4. Drag the Gallery's `FullImage` GameObject from the **Hierarchy** window to the **Full Image** field.
5. Drag the `Gallery`'s `Highlight` material from the **Project** window to the **Highlight Material** field.
6. Save the scene and project. Set the following values for each `Gallery`:
    - **(a)** Selected `Preview` GameObjects
    - **(b)** Add gallery title text
    - **(c)** Drag gallery text GameObject
    - **(d)** Drag `FullImage` GameObject
    - **(e)** Set **Hilight Material**:

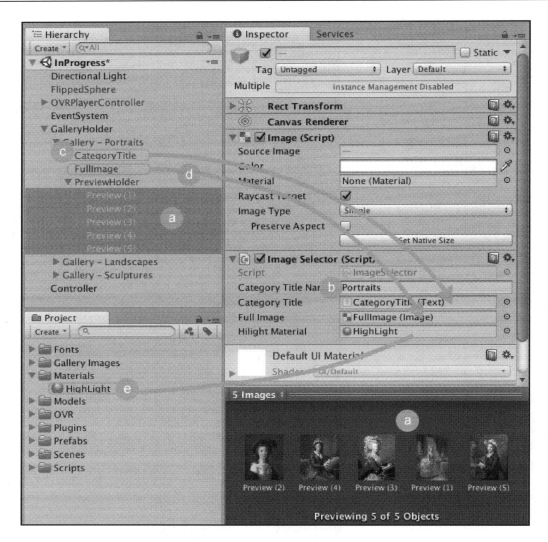

Figure 4.7: Setting the values for each Gallery

Finalizing user interaction

To complete our project, we will need to add two final components. These components will facilitate selecting an image for preview and providing visual feedback during the selection process.

Add the Graphic Raycaster component to the `Preview` objects. If you run the Scene, you will notice that our `Swipe` functions work as designed, but the user can not select a preview image for display. This is because our **Preview** thumbnail objects are looking for a Graphic Raycaster, but none is present; let's fix that:

1. Select `Preview (1)` through `Preview (5)` in the first Gallery `PreviewHolder`.
2. Click on **Add Component** in the **Inspector** window.
3. Search for `Graphic Raycaster` and apply it to the selected GameObject.
4. Repeat this process for each of the Gallery `PreviewHolders`.
5. Hit click on the Play button to test the interaction. While the scene is running, click on the **Preview** thumbnails to view a larger version of the image.
6. Save the scene and Unity project.
7. Navigate to **File | Save Scene** to create `WIP_6`.

Using Event Triggers for user feedback

Feedback is extremely important in every aspect of successful interactions. VR is no different. In Unity's Editor, it is very simple to select a thumbnail, because we have a visual pointing device (mouse), which makes the selection easy. In this VR environment, we do not have such a device, but we can still provide feedback to help guide the user.

The following steps will outline how to using Event Triggers to detect when the user's gaze has entered or left a thumbnail preview GameObject:

1. Select `Preview (1)` in the first `PreviewHolder` GameObject. Unfortunately, this operation can not be completed on multiple GameObjects at once.
2. Click on **Add Component** in the **Inspector** window and clear the search field.
3. Navigate to **Event | Event Trigger** and apply it to `Preview (1)`.
4. Click on the **Add New Event Type** button and choose select `PointerEnter`. This will create an empty Pointer Enter trigger list.
5. Click on the Plus symbol in the lower-right corner of the empty list to add a function to the empty list.
6. Drag the currently selected object, `Preview (1)`, from the **Hierarchy** window to replace the **None (Object)** value. By doing this, we are identifying `Preview (1)` as the object we want to manipulate.
7. The drop-down window with no function will be highlighted. Select navigate to **ImageSelector | OnPointerEnter (Image)** to assign the function.

8. Next, set the image value by dragging the **Image (Script)** component from higher up in the **Inspector** window to replace the **None (Image)** value. The value will change to `Preview (1)` (Image).

Test the change by clicking on the Play button to run the scene. While the scene is running, hover your cursor over the `Preview (1)` GameObject. Notice that it will now highlight as we defined in the script. However, it doesn't switch back to its default texture of none. So, we will add a new trigger to provide that feature:

1. Select the same `Preview (1)` GameObject.
2. Then, click on **Add New Event Type** under the Event Trigger component and choose `PointerExit`. The new event will be populated with the same values as the `Pointer Enter` event.
3. Change the drop-down function menu to **ImageSelector |
   OnPointerExit(Image)**.
4. Hit click on Play and test the event by hovering over the thumbnail with the mouse cursor.
5. Complete the feedback feature by adding these Event Triggers to each of the `Preview (x)` GameObjects.
6. Save the scene and Unity project.

Building the application

With our virtual gallery complete, it's time to build the application and install it on a mobile device for display in the Samsung Gear VR. The build process is exactly the same as building any other Android executable application.

Creating an osig file

Before the application can be installed, it must first be authorized by Oculus to run on the Gear VR. Skipping this step will result in an application that will run on the mobile device, but it will not be recognized when plugged into the Gear VR:

1. If you haven't done so, create an Oculus account at `https://developer.oculus.com/`. This step may have been completed when initially setting up the Gear VR device.
2. Obtain a **Device ID** and use it to generate an `.osig` file. This process can be completed at `https://dashboard.oculus.com/tools/osig-generator/`.
3. Navigate to the `project` folder in your OS and create the following folder path: `Assets/Plugins/Android/assets`.

4. Copy the `.osig` file created in Step 2 into the `Assets/Plugins/Android/assets` folder. It should be noted that you'll need to create a separate `.osig` file for each testing device. Each `.osig` file should be placed in this directory.

Preparing your Android device

Enable developer mode on your Android devices to gain access to USB debugging:

1. On your Android device, navigate to **Settings | About phone or Settings | About Device | Software Info**.
2. Scroll down to Build number and tap the item seven times. A popup will appear, confirming that you are now a developer.
3. Now, navigate to **Settings | Developer options | Debugging** and enable USB debugging.

Building an Android application

To build your application for Android, take the following steps:

1. Connect your Android device to the computer using a USB cable. You may see a prompt asking you to confirm that you wish to enable USB debugging on the device. If so, click **OK**.

2. In Unity, select **File** | **Build Settings** to load the **Build dialog**.

3. If it doesn't appear, add your current scene in the **Scenes In Build** portion of the dialog. This can be done by selecting the **Add Open Scenes**.

4. Change the platform to **Android** and click **Switch Platform**.

5. **Set Texture Compression** to ASTC.

6. Select **Player Settings...** and set the following attributes:
   - **Company Name**
   - **Product Name**
   - **Other Settings**
   - **Package Name**
   - **Minimal API Level**: API level 22
   - **XR Settings**
   - **Virtual Reality Supported: On**
   - **Virtual Reality SDK**: add Oculus

7. Click **Build and Run** to create an Android executable application and load it onto the mobile device:

Figure 4.8: Complete layout of Virtual Gallery

Summary

This project is a good introduction to creating interactions in VR. The use of a Raycaster and gaining input from the Gear VR trackpad are the hallmarks of many VR titles. For an extra challenge, try improving the project using the following suggestions or expand it with your own ideas:

- Arrange the galleries in a ring around the user and alter the `SwipeLeft` and `SwipeRight` to move the galleries along a circular path.
- Add a secondary text field that presents details such as the image title, artist's name, year produced, subject matter, medium, and details.
- Have the background change when the Raycaster focuses on a new gallery.

5
Fighting Zombies on the Oculus Rift

If opportunity doesn't knock, build a door.
- Milton Berle

This VR project will focus on developing an interactive game. The game is a first-person zombie shooter, built for the Oculus Rift; with slight modifications, it can also be compiled for the Google Cardboard, Daydream, or Samsung Gear VR.

Playing with zombies

Culturally, we've been fixated with the concept of shuffling hordes of undead creatures for decades. The subject of the undead has appeared in every entertainment platform to date: from print, to radio, to movies, to television, and finally to games. With this exposure, we have the luxury of not having to define the concept of a zombie. With so much interest, there is no lack of content to choose from. There are hundreds of free assets online and in the Asset Store for this genre. This will save us the considerable time and effort normally devoted to modeling, rigging, and animating the various components needed to build our experience.

Additionally, the video game shooter genre is so familiar that we'll have no trouble embellishing it to add our own creativity.

This game focuses on creating a stationary, first-person experience. The player is positioned at the junction of three alleyways and must destroy an unending stream of brain-thirsty zombies, armed with a gun.

Mac Users: At the time of this writing, the 1.20.0 release version of the Oculus Virtual Reality, OVR, plugin is not reliable on the Mac OS platform. Several developers, including myself, have run into problems getting Unity to load the plugin for standalone or Android builds. Staff members on the Unity forum have been alerted to the issue, but at present it remains low on their priority list. Because of this development, we would suggest waiting for a stable version of the plugin to be released before attempting this project on a Mac.

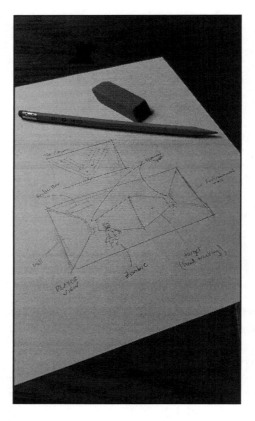

Figure 5.1: Environmental concept sketch

The Oculus Rift platform

While our previous projects have used mobile devices to deliver the VR experience, this project will focus on development of a desktop solution. The Oculus Rift (see Figure 5.2), or Rift, headset contains a stereoscopic **Organic Light-Emitting Diode** (**OLED**) display that produces a resolution of 1080x1200 within a 110° field of view. The headset is connected to a computer with a bundled USB and HDMI cable, tracking the user's head movements. Positioning is accomplished by IR LEDs embedded in the headset and stationary IR sensor(s). This means that VR applications for the Rift can be designed for a seated or room-scale experience.

Since the device is connected to a computer, our source content can be of a higher resolution and quality than could be handled by a mobile device, as we saw in the previous examples. All of this can be done in the Unity development with the addition of plugins and packages directly from Oculus:

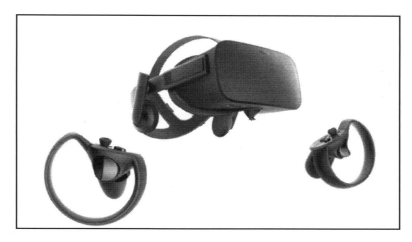

Figure 5.2: Oculus Rift Consumer version 1 headset with Touch controllers

Additionally, Oculus host a list of best practices when developing VR content on their website : `https://developer3.oculus.com/documentation/intro-vr/latest/`. Although we'll discuss many of these practices during this project, we suggest reviewing the complete list before planning your personal projects.

Process overview – Part 1

To build this zombie shooting range, we will split the work into several stages over two chapters. Part 1 will focus on the environment and the primary assets. These tasks are further divided into the following phases:

- Setting up the Unity environment
- Creating the player elements
- Building the game environment
- Creating the `Zombie` prefab

Once complete, we will move on to Part 2, where we will look at the scripts for zombie spawning, movement, attacking, and death. We will also use lighting and a skybox to set the mood, before learning how to build and deploy the final application. This will be a fun project, so sit back, fire up the latest version of Unity, and get ready to summon some *rotters*.

Setting up the Unity environment

To begin the project, we need to load the utility package and set a few variables within the Unity editor to establish that we are creating a VR project:

1. In `Chapter 3`, *Building an Image Gallery System for the Gear VR*, we loaded the Oculus Utilities from the **Asset Store**. As an alternative, for the plugin/package can also be acquired directly from the Oculus website. Visit `https://developer.oculus.com/downloads/unity/` and select the Oculus Utilities for Unity link to download the latest utility package. While Unity provides built-in VR support for both the Oculus Rift and the Samsung Gear VR, the scripts, assets, and prefabs contained in this plugin facilitate additional functionality. For more information, see the Unity Developer Guide at `https://developer.oculus.com/documentation/unity/latest/concepts/book-unity-gsg/`.
2. Locate the archive in your download location and decompress the file before continuing.
3. Launch Unity and create a new Unity project named `ZombieGame`.
4. Choose **Asset | Import Package | Custom Package** and select the `OculusUtilities.unitypackage` from the extracted archive folder.
5. Choose the **All** button to select the entire package, then scroll down and deselect the `Scenes` directory.

6. Click the **Import** buttons at the bottom of the window to import the package elements.

7. Click yes if Unity asks to update the Oculus Utilities Plugin. If an update is required, Unity will restart to install the required files.

Rather than creating our own creature, we will rely on a free zombie asset from the Unity **Asset Store** shown in Figure 5.3. This superb asset contains the model, materials, and animations needed to bring the game to life (pun intended).

8. Choose **Window | Asset Store** and search for `Zombie` and `Pxltiger` in the store. Select Import to download the assets from the store directly into your Unity project. The asset can be found here:

    `https://www.assetstore.unity3d.com/en/#!/content/30232:`

Figure 5.3: Zombie asset package in the Asset Store from Pxltiger

9. Add the following directories to the **Project** window: `Materials`, `Prefabs`, `Scenes`, `Scripts`, and `Sprites`.

10. Select the **Directional Light** and rename it `Production Lighting`. We use this title to denote that the light will be used in production, but will be deactivated or deleted from the final build.

11. Set the **Intensity** of `Production Lighting` to `0.5` and **Shadow Type** to **No Shadows** in the **Inspector** panel. In the end, we will turn off this light, but we are using it now to illuminate the scene as we construct the environment.

12. Open the **Lighting** panel from **Window** | **Lighting** | **Settings**. Dock the **Lighting** panel with the **Inspector** if it appears in a separate window. We will need this later in the project, when we set the scene's mood.

13. Use **File** | **Save Scene As...** to save the scene as `ShootingRange`. Save the scene into the `Scenes` directory or move it to the `Project/Scenes` folder in Unity.

Creating the Player GameObject

The player is made up of a single GameObject. This object will contain the first-person camera, a collider, and a light source. Our GameObject will not need a light source until we address the environment in the Setting the mood section, but we can create the other components by following the steps listed here:

1. Create an empty GameObject in the **Hierarchy** panel, rename it `Player`, and move it to `0,1,0.5` using the **Inspector**. This object will house the VR camera and scripts needed for player control.

2. Change the `Player` tag from `Untagged` to `Player` using the **Inspector** panel.

3. With the object still selected, add a Capsule Collider by clicking the **Add Component** button in the **Inspector** window. Enter `capsule` in the search field or select Physics from the list of categories. Next, select Capsule Collider from the list to assign it to the `Player` GameObject.

Unity Colliders are invisible objects used to facilitate physical collisions between GameObjects. They can be exact shapes or rough approximations of the object's mesh renderer and can be primitive or complex in definition. In normal operations, we use an object's collider to determine if two objects have touched and then act upon those results programmatically. In this project, the player's collider will collide with the ground so that we don't pass through the floor. It will also be used to trigger the zombie's attack animation after the two (player and zombie) collide.

4. Set the Capsule Collider's center z-value to −0.25 and increase the **Height** from 1 to 2.

Graphic Raycaster

To kill a zombie, our player will need the ability to shoot. We will cover this in detail in the next chapter, but it is important to note that we will not be firing a projectile from the Player GameObject. Instead, we will use a Physics Raycaster to direct a beam from the center of the user's point-of-view to a focus point in the distance. Think of the Raycaster as an invisible laser pointer that kills the first zombie it collides with.

Adding a 3D camera

A 3D camera will be used to provide the first-person view needed in a VR experience. It will also be the origin point for our graphic Raycaster. Before implementing the new camera, we need to delete the existing Main Camera GameObject:

1. Right-click the Main Camera item and choose **Delete**. Without a camera, Display 1 No camera rendering will be displayed in the **Game** window.
2. Navigate to the `Project/OVR/Prefab` directory and locate the `OVRCameraRig` prefab. Drag the `OVRCameraRig` to the `Player` GameObject. The `OVRCameraRig` will appear as a sub-item to the `Player`.
3. Move the camera (not the `Player` GameObject) to 0,0.5,0.
4. Save the `ShootingRange` scene.

Building the game environment

Next, we will create the GameObjects needed to establish our play area. Our player will be standing still, so our level design can be very simple. It will consist of a few walls, a ground plane, some spawn points for our shambling undead, and eventually a moody skydome. We'll start by creating a container to hold the physical boundaries of the space.

Constructing gameplay boundaries

In the game, our player will battle for their life from a stationary position. The scene is a typical unrealistic Hollywood back alley, which sits at the junction of three pathways. Every few seconds, a zombie will be spawned in one of the pathways and the creature will then move toward the player.

We need to create an environment that facilitates the zombie action while also focusing the player's attention on the task at hand. In the following steps, we will construct the scene elements needed to facilitate our gameplay. A ground plane and several cubes will be used to define boundaries for the gameplay:

1. Create an empty GameObject called `Environment`. Make sure it is sitting at `0,0,0.5`.
2. Add the following objects from the **GameObject | 3D Object** menu to the `Environment` GameObject and transform them, as indicated in *Table 5.1*:

Type	Name	Position			Rotation			Scale		
		X	Y	Z	X	Y	Z	X	Y	Z
Plane	Ground	0	0	22.5	0	0	0	6	1	6
Cubes	Left 1	-16	2	8.5	0	42	0	44	4	0.1
	Left 2	-18	2	15.8	0	40	0	40	4	0.1
	Left 3	-2.7	2	23	0	90	0	40	4	0.1
	Right 3	2.7	2	23	0	90	0	40	4	0.1
	Right 2	18	2	15.8	0	140	0	40	4	0.1
	Right 1	16.37	2	8.85	0	137	0	44	4	0.1

Table 5.1: GameObject attributes

Figure 5.4 is a screenshot of the scene which illustrates the layout so far. Feel free to tweak the environment to meet your needs. In our example, we have positioned the shooting alleys so that the action takes place in a 110° arc. This will allow for quick motions while limiting the effects of motion sickness for the VR player. The topic of combating motion sickness will be discussed in more detail in the next chapter.

In this image, we've set the Shading Mode to **Shaded Wireframe** to help differentiate each of the GameObjects. This will be helpful later when the atmospheric conditions are set:

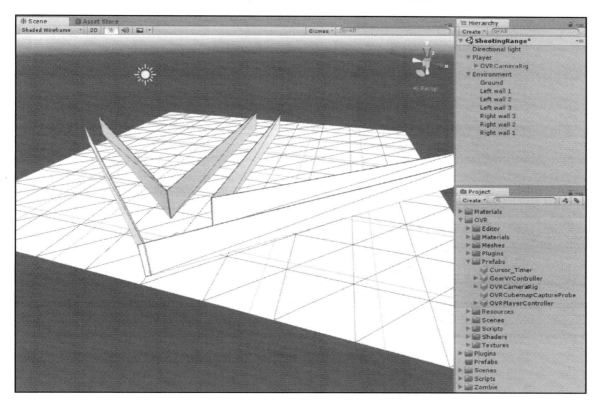

Figure 5.4: The scene environment (in Shaded Wireframe mode) including project folders

With the boundaries in place, we can test the environmental setup via the OVR camera. Hit the Play button (*Ctrl + P* or *command + P*) and put on the Rift headset to enter the scene.

3. Adjust the environment as needed.
4. Save the Scene.

Setting the mood

It's great to be able to see our scene in action, but the harsh lighting and grey walls don't really fit our zombie theme. We can correct that with a few materials and a new lighting setup:

1. Right-click in the **Project** panel and create two new materials.
2. Rename the materials Ground and Walls.
3. Set the color for both materials. Use darker colors for both, but the walls should be a bit brighter. We used hex values #514735FF for the Ground and #65615AFF for the Walls.

   Unity uses 4 pairs of hexadecimal values to specify color. The format for these values is #RRGGBBAA, where RR (red), GG (green), BB (blue) and AA (Alpha) are hexadecimal integers between 00 and FF specifying the intensity of the color.

   For example, #FF800000 is displayed as bright orange, because the red component is set to its highest value (FF), the green is set to a medium value (80), and the others are set to 00.

   When creating transparent colors, set the AA (Alpha) to a value less than FF and the material's **Render Mode** to **Transparent**.

4. Use the Inspector to set the **Smoothness** to 0 and turn off the **Specular Highlights** for both materials. Add the new materials to the Materials folder and apply the Ground and Walls materials to the respective objects.
5. Choose Spotlight from the **GameObject | Light** menu to add a new Spotlight to the scene.
6. Rename the new light Flashlight.
7. Make the Flashlight a child of the camera rig. To do this, drag the Flashlight asset to Player/OVRCameraRig/TrackingSpace/CenterEyeAnchor in the **Hierarchy** panel.
8. Set the Flashlight's attributes to the following: **Position** 0,0,0; **Rotation** 0,0,0; **Spot Angle** 55; **Intensity** 2.
9. Put on the headset again and hit the Play button. Adjust the materials or Flashlight as needed.
10. Save the ShootingRange scene.

Creating spawn points

When completed, our game will spawn a new zombie every five seconds at one of three spawn points. Each undead creature will then shamble toward the player to attack and consume a fresh brain. For the next step, we'll create and position three spawn points within our scene:

1. Create three empty GameObjects, naming each one `ZombieSpawnPoint` and position them as indicated in *Table 5.2*:

	Position		
Name	X	Y	Z
ZombieSpawnPoint	-23	0	17
ZombieSpawnPoint	0	0	23
ZombieSpawnPoint	23	0	17

Table 5.2: Spawner positions

2. Select one of the `ZombieSpawnPoint`'s. In the **Inspector**, click on the Tag dropdown and choose **Add Tag...**, this will open the **Tags & Layers** panel. The Tag list will be identified as List is Empty. Click the + symbol to add a new tag called `SpawnPoint`.

3. Use *Shift* + select to select the `ZombieSpawnPoint`'s and assign the new tag. The result should be that each spawn point has the `SpawnPoint` tag. This tag will be used to randomly select a position when spawning `Zombies`.

4. Save the `ShootingRange` scene:

Figure 5.5: Updated environment

Optimizing the experience for VR

Your VR experience will only be pleasing if it is comfortable for the user. Nausea, dizziness, and malaise point to common reasons for VR discomfort and project failure. These issues result from poor planning and optimization of the experience.

Optimizing your VR project involves preparing your environment, graphics, and processes to run smoothly on the intended device. Unity maintains a list of resources and techniques for getting the most out of the Engine. Visit the link `https://unity3d.com/learn/tutorials/topics/virtual-reality/optimisation-vr-unit y` for an extensive look at the performance attributes to consider during development. For the purpose of this book we would like to discuss three key areas; frame rate, geometry reduction, and lightmapping.

Frame rate is key to performance

Each device has its own target frame rate, which has been thoroughly researched for the best performance. Most video games play at 30 frames per second, 30 fps for VR creates a visual lag, which causes discomfort and induces simulation sickness (see *Combating sickness* in `Chapter 7`, *Carnival Midway – Games Part 1*, for a detailed explanation on motion and simulation sickness). To avoid this problem, be sure your target device can display at least 60 fps.

Listed here are the frame rates for some popular devices:

- Device frame rates
- iPhone 4, Samsung Galaxy 5S: 30 fps
- Google Daydream: 50 fps
- Samsung Gear VR (and most mobile devices): 60 fps
- Oculus Rift and HTC Vive: 75-90 fps

Knowing the frame rate is only part of the issue. You also have to know the frame rate of your Unity scene. This can be done using the **Window** | **Profiler** panel. The Profiler lets you assess the performance of scene objects. From here, you can adjust specific objects for performance. View Unity's Live Training session on the Profiler (https://www.youtube.com/watch?v=tdGvsoASS3g) for more information on the diagnostic process and the Unite Europe session on Optimizing Mobile Applications (https://www.youtube.com/watch?v=j4YAY36xjwE).

Reducing excessive scene geometry

Realize that your device is doing double duty, because it is drawing each frame twice; once for the left eye and again for the right. This extra work is being done for every pixel in your scene. By default, it also applies to objects not currently in view by the camera. As your projects increase in size and complexity, reducing the extra load on the processor is important for keeping the frame rate high enough for a comfortable VR experience. Currently, there are a few primary methods for reducing the processor's workload; removing objects that will never be in view, using single-sided GameObjects, and using occlusion culling.

Removing unnecessary objects

This is the first pass. If objects will never be seen by the user they should be removed. Unity is smart enough to ignore these objects, but this technique will also reduce the final application size. Likewise, if only part of an object is visible, the object should be modified so that only the visible parts are within the scene.

Using planes

Planes are single-sided 3D objects which can be colored with materials or textured with Sprites. Being single-sided means that rendering resources are not used to represent the other side of the object. When used in the background or on distant objects we can create the appearance of 3D details by using 2D shapes. This is another method for reducing unnecessary geometry.

Occlusion culling

By default, Unity only renders objects viewable within the camera's field of view. This is called Frustum Culling and is very common in computer rendering. Occlusion culling is a feature where Unity disables rendering of GameObjects obscured by other objects.

The following image illustrates the difference:

Figure 5.6: Left: Normal scene, no culling
Middle: Frustum culling, only objects within the camera's viewing cone are rendered
Right: Occlusion culling, obscured objects are not rendered

Occlusion culling will not be needed for our simple scene, but larger game environments with many areas are often hampered by performance issues. If this occurs in your environment, try setting up occlusion culling. It is very simple and will greatly improve performance. See the following link for more information: https://docs.unity3d.com/Manual/OcclusionCulling.html.

Lightmapping

There are two types of lighting systems in Unity: real-time or precomputed which can be used in combination. Whenever possible, it's best to eliminate dynamic lighting and real-time shadows and incorporate precomputed baked lighting. See the Unity guide to Lighting and Rendering `https://unity3d.com/learn/tutorials/modules/beginner/graphics/lighting-and-rendering`, **for more information:** `https://unity3d.com/learn/tutorials/topics/graphics/introduction-lighting-and-rendering`.

Although our small scene will not need any optimization, this is a step that should be considered on all projects:

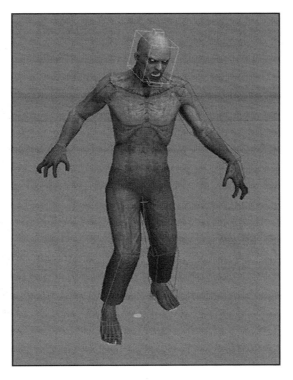

Figure 5.7: Walking animation from Zombie GameObject

Let's get back to the project. Our next step is to create a zombie prefab and a system to control the zombie's behavior. The asset we downloaded has five different animations: walking, attacking, and the three dying animations (falling back, falling right, and falling left).We'll need a method for calling those animations when specific events occur. To do that, we'll use the Animator Controller.

The Animator Controller is a state machine. Like a flowchart, this state machine illustrates how various animations are linked to different actions. A state refers to the action a GameObject is currently engaged in: things like walking, jumping, or running. The state machine makes it easier to keep track of the actions and their associated variables, and creates a mechanism for transitioning from one state to another.

Creating the zombie prefab

We can now begin the process of incorporating the Zombies into our scene. The Zombie asset created by Pxltiger comes with the models, materials, textures, and animated prefabs. This saves us hours of work constructing the elements, but we still need to prepare the assets for our scene and create a means of controlling the various states needed to have the creature interact with our player:

1. Create the `Zombie` prefab by dragging the `Zombie/Model/z@walk` asset from the **Project** window to the **Hierarchy** window. When the item appears in the **Hierarchy** panel, the text will be blue.

   We are utilizing the walk animation since our *biters* will always be moving. For future projects, you might want to use an idle or default animation as the project requires.

2. Rename the `z@walk` item to `ZombiePrefab` in the **Inspector** panel.
3. Add a Capsule Collider component to the prefab item with the following settings:
   - Center=0,0.85,0.3
   - Radius=0.17
   - Height=1.7

4. Add a Rigidbody component.

   Adding the Rigidbody component to an object will subject the object to Unity's physics engine. With this component, vector forces and gravity can be used to simulate behaviors. The Rigidbody component will let objects fall, roll, and bounce in a manner that we would expect in the real world.

5. Change **Collision Detection** to **Continous Dynamic**.
6. Set constraints Freeze Position Y = On.
7. Set constraints Rotation X = On and Z = On.
8. Drag the `ZombiePrefab` from the **Hierarchy** panel to the `Prefabs` folder. This will create a new prefab.
9. With the new prefab created, delete the `ZombiePrefab` item from the **Hierarchy** panel.

Before the zombies can be spawned, we need to create a state machine to control their animations (walking, attacking, and dying). This state machine is created with the Animator tool. If you have not used the Animator, Unity has provided a short video introduction to the tool: `https://unity3d.com/learn/tutorials/topics/animation/animator-controller`. The following steps illustrate how to create a state machine for our asset.

Animating the zombie assets

Take the following steps to animate the zombie assets:

1. Choose **Asset** | **Create** | **Animator Controller** from the main menu.
2. Rename the new asset `ZombieAnimator` and place it in the `Project/Zombie` folder.

3. Double-click the `ZombieAnimator` to load the state engine into the **Animator** window for editing:

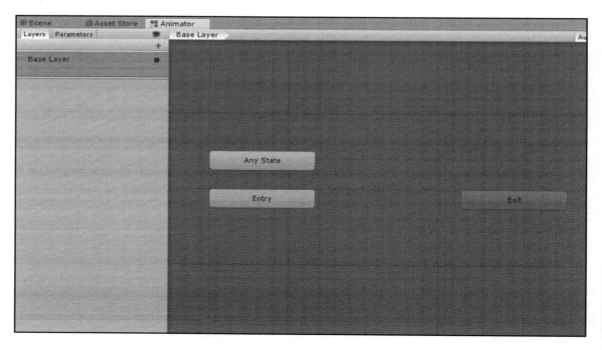

Figure 5.8: Based on the size of your display, you may have to pan around (MMB+drag) the window to locate the three states

Within the window we will define three parameters, five states, and seven transitions, which will be used to control the behaviors and actions of our zombie horde. The state machine is useful because it creates a smooth seamless transition between the asset's animations.

4. With the **Animator** window open, select the **Parameter** tab and create the following items by choosing `Bool` or `Int` from the + menu:
    1. `Death` (Boolean): used to determine if the Zombie can move or attack
    2. `Attack` (Boolean): used to determine if the Zombie is attacking
    3. `DeathAnimationIndex` (Integer): used to determine which death animation will be played.

5. Create five new states by right-clicking on an empty spot in the grey grid area and choosing Create **State** | **Empty**. Rename the items `Walk`, `Attack`, `FallLeft`, `FallRight`, and `FallBack` in the **Inspector** panel.

FallLeft, FallRight, and FallBack are the zombie's three death animations. They indicate the direction of the death, such as fall straight back, fall back to the left and fall back to the right.

6. Confirm that the Walk state is the default by right-clicking on Walk and choosing **Set as Layer Default State**.

7. Right-click the Walk state and select **Make Transition**. Then click on Attack to anchor the transition. When called from a script, this transition will create a smooth blending between the walk cycle and the attack animations. If you make a mistake, select the state in the **Animator** window and the **Transition** in the **Inspector** panel. Then, hit the - button in the lower corner to remove the transition.

8. Continue by adding transitions, as indicated in the following image. When completed, Walk will be the starting point for four transitions, Attack will start three, and the remaining items (FallLeft, FallRight, and FallBack) start zero transitions. *Figure 5.9* illustrates the **Animator** layout when you've completed this step:

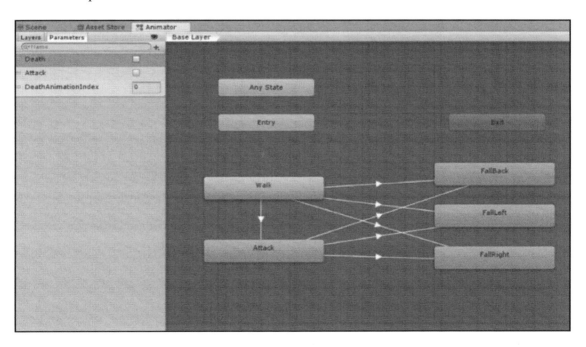

Figure 5.9: Layout of states for the ZombieAnimator

9. Select the `Walk` item and review the **Inspector** window. Note that the **Motion** field has a value of **None (Motion)**. Change this by clicking the small target selector circle and choosing walk from the Select Motion dialog. The items listed here were created by the zombie asset creator and will save us the time of animating them ourselves. Complete this step by selecting each of the other states and setting their motion to the appropriate animation.

10. Save the `ShootingRange` scene.

Adding transitions

Next, we need to set the condition for each transition. The condition decides when a zombie transitions from one state to another, such as from walking to attacking. For our game, we have seven transitions, as shown in *Table 5.3*. A zombie's starting state is walking and it transitions to either attacking or dying, depending on whether it collides with the player or the Raycaster. If it collides with the Raycaster, the transition is one of the three death animations. If it collides with the player, then it plays an attack before switching to a death:

1. Select a transition arrow and review its settings in the **Inspector** window. Note that at the bottom of the window the Condition panel is empty. Add a condition to each transition by clicking the + button and complete the fields by using the following chart. Additionally, be sure to uncheck the **Has Exit Time** checkbox for each transition. *Table 5.3* outlines the `Attack`, `Death`, and `DeathAnimationIndex` values for each transition:

Transition	Has Exit Time	Conditions
Walk->Attack		Attack is **True**
Walk->Fallback		Death is **True** `DeathAnimationIndex` **Equals** 0
Walk->FallLeft		Death is **True** `DeathAnimationIndex` **Equals** 1
Walk->FallRight	**False**	Death is **True** `DeathAnimationIndex` **Equals** 2
Attack->Fallback		Death is **True** `DeathAnimationIndex` **Equals** 0
Attack->FallLeft		Death is **True** `DeathAnimationIndex` **Equals** 1
Attack->FallRight		Death is **True** `DeathAnimationIndex` **Equals** 2

Table 5.3: Condition settings for each transition

Thankfully, the `Zombie` asset came with these animations. They'll work perfectly for our project with one minor tweak. The current walk cycle animates for a single stride. However, to have our undead creatures move naturally toward the player, we'll need a full stride that repeats the entire duration of the movement.

2. Double-click the Walk state in the **Animator** window. This will open the object in the **Inspector** panel.

3. Choose the **Animation** button (see *Figure 5.10*) and scroll down to the walk animation section. Convert the animation to a walk cycle by checking the **Loop Time** option.

4. Hit the **Apply** button to save the change:

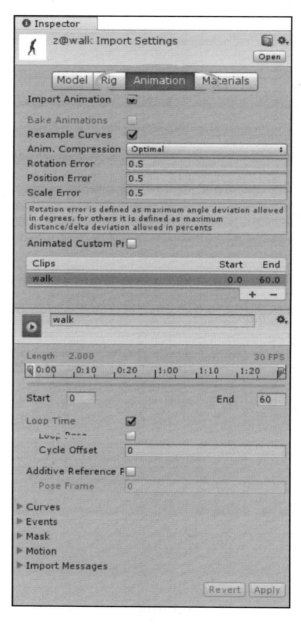

Figure 5.10: Looping the walk animation

Now that the `ZombieAnimator` has been created, we can assign the state machine to the `ZombiePrefab`.

5. Select the `ZombiePrefab` and note that the **Controller** field in the **Inspector** panel is set the **None (Runtime Animator Controller)**.
6. Click the target selector on the **Controller** field and select the `ZombieAnimator` from the Select **Runtime Animator Controller** window.
7. Save the `ShootingRange` scene and the project.

Summary

We have now completed the setup phase of this project. Our scene provides an environment for the zombie animator and spawn points. Donning the headset and hitting play will let you look around the space, but we still will not see any creatures making their way toward the player. To get them started, we need to create three new scripts: the `PlayerController`, the `ZombieController`, and the `ZombieSpawner`. Each of these scripts will be covered in detail in the next chapter.

Another important component of this chapter was the discussion on creating comfortable experiences in virtual reality. Optimizing your project is centered around making development choices based on your target device. Visit Unity's VR tutorials at https://unity3d.com/learn/tutorials/topics/virtual-reality/optimisation-vr-unity, for a detailed list of resources and techniques to make your projects run smoothly. Although we have not implemented forced player movement, it is best to be aware of the optimization practices and how they can affect our players.

6
Scripting Zombies for the Oculus Rift

"You can't use up creativity. The more you use, the more you have."

- Maya Angelou

With the environment and primary assets in place, we can now focus on the programmatic side of the project. This second part of our development process will involve the following phases:

- Scripting the zombies
- Controlling the `Zombie` prefab
- Building a `PlayerController` script
- Setting the mood
- Building an executable
- Expanding the experience
- Summary

Scripting the zombies

In this chapter, we'll finish up the ShootingRange project with scripts and interactivity. Keep in mind that the approach we're taking is just a guide; it's designed to be embellished with your own creativity with regards to the environment and interactions in the world. So, with that said, let's get back to the action.

Summoning zombies

In Chapter 6, *Scripting Zombies for the Oculus Rift*, we constructed the scene, which included the environment, the Zombie prefab, and a state machine to control the animations. We can now create the scripts needed to spawn enemies at the ZombieSpawnPoint GameObjects.

ZombieSpawner script

The ZombieSpawner is a simple script that randomly instantiates a zombie at one of the three ZombieSpawnPoint points every few seconds. Take the following steps to set it up:

1. Create an empty GameObject named SpawnController and position it anywhere in the scene. I generally like to put controller scripts at 0,0,0, but since our player will be anchored to that location, feel free to place it somewhere else. Try using 0,0,-2 for this example.
2. Add a new script to the SpawnController and name it ZombieSpawner.
3. Move the script to our Scripts folder.
4. Double-click the script to launch it in your editor. Edit the script to match the following:

```
using System.Collections;
using System.Collections.Generic;
using UnityEngine;

public class ZombieSpawner : MonoBehaviour {
    public GameObject zombiePrefab;
    public float zombieSpawnFrequency; // controls how often
zombies appear

    // Use this for initialization
    IEnumerator Start () {
        while (true) {
            GameObject zombie = Instantiate (zombiePrefab);
```

```
GameObject [] zombieSpawners =
GameObject.FindGameObjectsWithTag ("SpawnPoint");

zombie.transform.position = zombieSpawners
[Random.Range (0,
zombieSpawners.Length)].transform.position;
yield return new WaitForSeconds
(zombieSpawnFrequency);
        }
    }
}
```

In this script, we've created two public variables: `zombiePrefab` and `zombieSpawnFrequency`. Like the other variables, we've tried to use descriptive names to indicate their function. The `zombiePrefab` will be used to determine which GameObject should be spawned. Here, we are only using one type of zombie, but your project might require different prefabs being spawned from different locations.

`zombieSpawnFrequency` is used to determine how often the creatures are summoned from their eternal rest to seek unholy vengeance on the living. During testing, you'll want to adjust this value to meet your needs.

After assigning values to these variables, we want the script to start running. You'll notice that, instead of `void Start()`, we've utilized `IEnumerator Start ()`.

Typically, a function will run to completion in a single frame. All commands are evaluated and compiled, then the screen refreshes to show the results. When a script calls for a visual change over time (such as fading the screen, animating an item, and so on) you'll probably want to use a coroutine.

 A coroutine is like a function that has the ability to pause execution and return control to Unity, but also to continue where it left off in the following frame.

The IEnumerator allows us to start the spawning process, yield control back to Unity, and then pick up again where we left off in the next frame. Using this method will properly display animations and visual effects over time.

The meat of this script is within a `while` loop. The loop creates a new zombie instance called zombie. This instance is our previously defined prefab with all of its features and attributes, including the animations and state machine. Next, a list of spawn points is created by searching for GameObjects with tags set to `SpawnPoint`. A random point from that list is then selected and used as the location for the zombie instance. Once that is completed, the script waits for a number of seconds equal to the `zombieSpawnFrequency` variable:

1. Save the script and return to Unity.
2. Make sure the `SpawnController` is selected and note that the new `Zombie` Prefab field has a value of None (GameObject). Click the target selector circle next to the Zombie Prefab field and select the `ZombiePrefab` GameObject created in *Chapter 6*, *Scripting Zombies for the Oculus Rift*, by double-clicking. Alternatively, you could drag the GameObject from the `Prefab` folder to this field.
3. Set the **Zombie Spawn Frequency** to five. This is only a default value, so feel free to change it after testing the scene.
4. Save the scene, hit Play and put on the headset.

At this point, we should have an environment where the player can look around. It's probably a little too bright, so go back and turn off the `Production Lighting` GameObject. The mood isn't perfect, but we'll address that later. You'll also notice that our zombies are spawning at a rate of one every five seconds, but they are not moving toward the player. They are fixed at their randomly selected spawn location facing the wrong direction. We will address these next in the `Zombie Controller` script.

Controlling the zombie prefab

This next script manages zombie behavior. With it in place, a spawned zombie will:

- Turn toward the player and start walking
- Move at a predetermined speed
- Die at the appropriate times
- Randomly choose one of the three death animations: `FallBack`, `FallLeft`, or `FallRight`

ZombieController script

This script will be attached to the `ZombiePrefab` so that the behavior is applied each time an animated corpse is spawned. Take the following steps to set it up:

1. Select the `ZombiePrefab` from the `Project/Prefab` folder and add a script component in the **Inspector** panel. Rename the script `ZombieController`.

2. Move the script to the `Scripts` folder.

3. Open the script in your editor and remove the `Start ()` function. Since this script is a little longer, we'll break the description into parts:

```
using System.Collections;
using System.Collections.Generic;
using UnityEngine;

public class ZombieController : MonoBehaviour {
    private Animator _animator;
    private Rigidbody _rigidbody;
    private CapsuleCollider _collider;
    private GameObject _target;

    public float moveSpeed = 1.5f;
    private bool _isDead, _isAttacking;
```

The `ZombieController` script will primarily handle the prefab's movement, attack, and death. This first bit of code is used to create and assign values to the local variables:

```
private void Awake () {
    // Awake occurs when a zombie is spawned. At that time we capture
    prefab components
    // for use in movement, collision, attack and death
    _animator = GetComponent<Animator> ();
    _rigidbody = GetComponent<Rigidbody> ();
    _collider = GetComponent<CapsuleCollider> ();
    _target = GameObject.FindGameObjectWithTag("Player");
}

private void Update () {
    // During each frame we rotate the zombie toward the player. This
    allows for player
    // movement during runtime
    Vector3 targetPostition = new Vector3(
    _target.transform.position.x,
    0f, _target.transform.position.z );
    transform.LookAt (targetPostition);
}
```

```
private void FixedUpdate () {
    // In FixedUpdate we move the prefab, if it is alive and not
    attacking
    if (!_isDead && !_isAttacking) {
    _rigidbody.velocity = (_target.transform.position -
    transform.position).normalized * moveSpeed;
        }
}
```

Here, we call three methods, `Awake`, `Update`, and `FixedUpdate`, to access different components of the prefab. In `Awake`, we assign component values to the four private variables.

After being spawned, our zombies are going to move in a straight line toward the player. However, since the left and right lane are at an angle, this could produce an unwanted situation where the zombies are moving in one direction, but facing another. To fix this, we add a `LookAt`. This command rotates the prefab's transform so that the forward vector points to a specific object or location. In this case, we are pointing them toward the player's location within the scene.

Where `Update` rotates the prefab toward the player GameObject, `FixedUpdate` moves our zombie. The `if` statement is used to determine if the creature should be moving. When this statement is true, the `Zombie` prefab moves toward the origin (the player's starting position) based on the provided **Move Speed**. Note that the z-value of the spawn points if either `17` or `23`, and to move towards the player we need a negative velocity.

We use `FixedUpdate` here because it is called in regular interval where `Update` runs after all calculations are completed. Because of this, `Time.deltaTime` for `Update` is varied, where as, `Time.deltaTime` for `FixedUpdate` is consistent.

> `FixedUpdate` should be used instead of `Update` when dealing with Rigidbody: `https://docs.unity3d.com/ScriptReference/Rigidbody.html`. For example, when adding a force to a Rigidbody, you have to apply the force to every fixed frame inside `FixedUpdate` instead of every frame inside `Update`.

The next two functions will determine what happens when a zombie is killed:

```
public void Die () {
    // Once we have decided to kill off a zombie, we must set its local
    // variables to their default values.
    _rigidbody.velocity = Vector3.zero;
    _collider.enabled = false;
    _isDead = true;
```

```
        _animator.SetBool ("Death", true);
        _animator.SetInteger ("DeathAnimationIndex", Random.Range (0, 3));
        StartCoroutine (DestroyThis ());
    }

    IEnumerator DestroyThis () {
        // Before destroying the prefab, we will wait until it's animation
        is complete
        // the value listed here is the length of the walk cycle
        yield return new WaitForSeconds (1.5f);
        Destroy (GameObject);
    }
```

Let's look at the individual statements in void Die to get a better understanding of what is going on in this script.

The first statement sets the prefab's velocity to zero, stopping the zombie's forward motion. Then, we turn off the collider. By turning off the collider, we are assured the prefab can no longer trigger actions associated with the raycaster or the player.

Next, we set the _isDead variable to true signifying that the zombie should no longer be treated as a threat, that is capable of attacking the player. The following two lines set the Animator's Death parameter to true and plays a random death animation. Once the animation begins, we call another coroutine called DestoryThis. This coroutine then waits for 1.5 seconds (the length of the death animations) before removing the GameObject from the scene.

Make sure the script has a closing } bracket:

1. Save the script, return to Unity.
2. Run the scene.

We now have the base structure for our zombie controller, but we still need to add a few more functions. As the scene runs, the zombies will spawn as indicated by the frequency setting and move toward the player using the **Move Speed** value.

However, since we do not have a method for triggering the `Die()` function, our scene will continually spawn zombies, overrunning the player and filling the space:

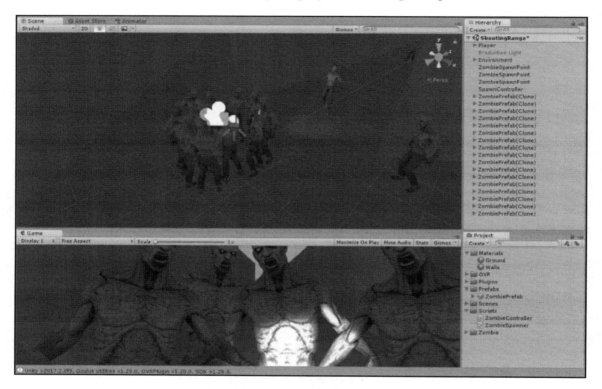

Figure 6.1: Zombies on the march

Fighting back

The `PlayerController` will let the Player interact with the game world. With it, we will provide a shooting mechanic which involves displaying a target, listening for user input, and generating a raycaster to intersect with the shambling horde.

PlayerController script

Take the following steps to set up the `PlayerController` script:

1. Select the `Player` GameObject and add a new script component. Name the script `PlayerController`.
2. Drag the `PlayerController` script from the `Project` folder to the `Project/Scripts` folder for organization.
3. Double-click the script to launch it in your editor.
4. Remove the `Start ()` function, as we've done in the past, and edit the file to match the following script:

```
using System.Collections;
using System.Collections.Generic;
using UnityEngine;

public class PlayerController : MonoBehaviour {
Vector3 hitPoint = new Vector3 (0, 1, 0);

void Update () {
// This statement checks to see if the primary Fire button has been
pressed
    if (Input.GetButtonDown ("Fire1")) {
        Shoot ();
    }
}

// This function casts a ray to determine when/if a zombie has been
hit
// on a successful hit the value of z will be the name of the
GameObject
 void Shoot () {
    RaycastHit hit;
    if (Physics.Raycast(Camera.main.transform.position,
    Camera.main.transform.forward, out hit)) {
        hitPoint = hit.point;
        ZombieController z =
        hit.collider.GetComponent<ZombieController> ();
        if (z != null)
        z.Die ();
    }
 }

// The Gizmos is an optional visual aid to help debug any targeting
issues with the Raycaster
```

```
private void OnDrawGizmos () {
        Gizmos.color = Color.red;
        Gizmos.DrawLine (hitPoint, Camera.main.transform.position);
    }
}
```

Update function

Statements in the Update () function are called in each frame that the scene is running. In our function, we are listening for input from the Player. If the Player clicks the left mouse button, or presses the *A* or *X* buttons on the Touch controller, the Shoot () function will run. Keep in mind that interaction with a button can have three stages. First, the Touch controller has sensors which detect when fingers are near a button. Second, a button can be pressed. Third, a button can be released. In each of these cases, we can trigger an event to coincide with player interaction.

So, the GetButtonDown call will be true for the Update frame while the button is being pressed. It will revert to false at the start of the next frame.

Shoot function

The Shoot () function, defined in the previous code block, runs for any frame where the Fire1 button has been pressed. The functions purpose is to simulate the Player shooting a weapon at a zombie. Instead of a projectile, we are instantiating a graphic Raycaster.

In the script you will notice that a ray called hit is created. This ray will be used to determine the trajectory of an imaginary bullet when the Fire1 button is released. The ray is drawn in the forward direction starting from the OVRCameraRig's current position. If the ray intersects with a collider attached to a zombie prefab, then a hit is recorded and the zombie dies.

OnDrawGizmos function

The last function is an optional visual aid used primarily for debugging. Gizmos are very useful for visualizing vector information. In this case, we are using a red GizmoDrawLine to illustrate the direction of the hit ray:

- Save the script and return to Unity.

Testing the PlayerController

Hit the Play button the test the scene. Clicking the left mouse button or *A* or *X* on the Touch controller will display a ray in the **Scene** window. `Zombies` that collide with the ray will die.

Everything is working well expect for two things:

1. The zombies never attack the player
2. Without visual feedback

it's almost impossible to tell if you've lined up your shot. So, let's address these last two things as we wrap up the project:

1. Reopen the `zombieController` script.
2. Inject the following functions at the end of the script. before the last curly bracket. to facilitate the zombie attack function:

```
private void OnCollisionEnter (Collision other) {
// This code will initiate an attack when the player GameObject
intersects
// with a zombie collider
if (other.collider.tag == "Player" && !_isDead) {
        StartCoroutine(Attack
        (other.collider.GameObject.GetComponent<PlayerController>
()));
    }
}

IEnumerator Attack (PlayerController player) {
        _isAttacking = true;
        _animator.SetBool ("Attack", true);
        yield return new WaitForSeconds (44f / 30f);
        Die ();
}
```

In our game, a zombie attack occurs when the prefab's capsule collider begins touching the player's capsule collider. This interaction is determined by the `OnCollisionEnter()` which seeks to collect data using `other.collider`. In this case, we are checking that the other GameObject is tagged as `Player`.

Additionally, the `if` statement makes sure the zombie's `_isDead` attribute is false. If this were not the case then, once the zombie collided, it would continue to attack until killed, which is what would happen in the real world, but is not needed for our simulation.

Inside of the `if` statement is our final coroutine. Here, we are mimicking the coroutine relationship between `Die()` and `DestroyThis()` by having an `Attack()` function kicked off by the `OnCollisionEnter()` function. The only difference is that, in this case, we are also passing along player information.

The final function defines `Attack(PlayerController player)` which, as previously stated, is called as a coroutine when a prefab collides with the `player` GameObject. Here, we set the prefab's `_isAttacking` attribute to true along with the Animator's Attack parameter. The `WaitForSeconds` statement is used to make sure the attack animation is completed before the final statement destroys the prefab.

The last step before closing the script is to make sure all curly brackets, { }, are properly closed.

3. Save the script, return to Unity and play the scene.

    At this point, the zombies spawn and move toward the player. They die when we shoot them or after they attack. Unfortunately, it is difficult to determine exactly where our shots will land. We will fix this by adding a targeting graphic to the player's view.

4. Stop the game before adding a targeting sprite to the `Player` GameObject.

Targeting reticle cursor

In the real world, reticles are used in microscopes and telescopes as a sighting aid. In games and VR, we use it for the same purpose, but we have a slightly different approach to their implementation. In 2D games, we can get away with attaching a sprite to the primary point-of-view camera. This works well in those instances because the player rarely needs to adjust between near and far objects. However, in VR titles, our player will need to switch focus between objects near and far. Attaching a sprite to the `OVRCamerRig` will cause double-vision as the player shifts focus between the reticle and the environment. This is known as voluntary diplopia and besides, being annoying, it causes headaches for some players.

The following steps outline a process for creating a reticle that uses the z-distance to help our player line up a shot. This eliminates the need for shifting focus because the reticle will be displayed on environmental objects:

1. From the **Hierarchy** panel select the `Player` GameObject and drill down to the `OVRCameraRig/TrackingSpace/CenterEyeAnchor` GameObject.

2. Right-click `CenterEyeAnchor` and select **UI | Canvas**. This will create a new UI Canvas as a child of the `CenterEyeAnchor` GameObject. We will use it as a container for the `Reticle`.

3. Rename the item `Cursor` and change the **Render Mode** to **World Space**.

4. Drag the `CenterEyeAnchor` GameObject to the **Event Camera** field in the Canvas component.

5. Go back up to the **Rect Transform** and set the values to the following:
   - **Pos X** = 0
   - **Pos Y** = 0
   - **Pos Z** = 0.3
   - **Height** = 100
   - **Width** = 100
   - **Rotation** = (0, 0, 0)
   - **Scale** = (0.001, 0.001, 0.001)

6. Right-click the `Cursor` GameObject and add a **UI | Image** element.

7. Rename the new `Image` object `Reticle` and set the **Rect Transform** to the following:
   - **Width** = 8
   - **Height** = 8
   - **Scale** = 0.1

8. Click the **Source Image** target selector and choose **None**, for a square shape or experiment with the other 2D Sprites listed. Additionally, you could create and import your own custom made `.png`.

9. Once a source is selected, use the **Color** field to set a color for your object.

10. Lastly, set the **Image Type** to **Simple**.

Figure 6.2 is a reference image of the **Inspector** panels for the `Cursor` and `Reticle` GameObjects. The values presented here are rough estimates. Be sure to test and adjust these values in your scene:

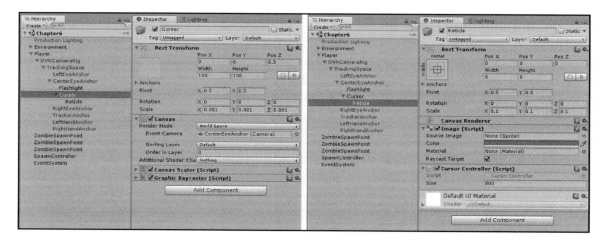

Figure 6.2: Cursor (UI Canvas) and Reticle (UI Image) settings

11. Click the **Add Component** button and add a new script called `CursorController`.

With both GameObjects in place, we can move on to the cursor script. The primary function of this script is the `Physics Raycast`. It is identical to the version created in the `PlayerController`, but here we are using it to determine which object is being gazed upon.

12. Double-click `CursorController` to edit the new script to match the following code:

```
using System.Collections;
using System.Collections.Generic;
using UnityEngine;

public class CursorController : MonoBehaviour {
    [SerializeField] float size = 800f;

    // Update is called once per frame
    void Update () {
```

```
RaycastHit hitInfo;
if (Physics.Raycast (Camera.main.transform.position,
Camera.main.transform.forward, out hitInfo)) {
    RectTransform rt = GetComponent<RectTransform> ();
    // when the raycast hits an object, these statements
    will transform the reticle to
    // match the illustrate the depth and rotation of the
    hit spot
    rt.position = hitInfo.point + (hitInfo.normal * 0.1f);
    rt.transform.rotation = Quaternion.FromToRotation
    (transform.forward, hitInfo.normal) *
    transform.rotation;
}

Vector3 a = Camera.main.WorldToScreenPoint
(transform.position);
Vector3 b = new Vector3 (a.x, a.y + size, a.z);

Vector3 aa = Camera.main.ScreenToWorldPoint (a);
Vector3 bb = Camera.main.ScreenToWorldPoint (b);

transform.localScale = Vector3.one * (aa - bb).magnitude;
    }
}
```

Overall, this code uses a Physics Raycaster to find GameObjects within the scene. When an object collides with the raycaster, we resize and rotate the Source Image at the point of intersection. This gives us a reticle that tracks the player's head movement within the environment, providing a targeting point that matches the position used in the `Shoot ()` function in `PlayerController`. Personally, I think this is a better solution than the traditional 2D sprite component we find in most games.

For another approach to building VR-applicable reticles, try the `VRInteractiveItem` script from Unity (`https://unity3d.com/learn/tutorials/topics/virtual-reality/interaction-vr`) or the in-depth reticle tutorial (`https://www.youtube.com/watch?v=LLKYbwNnKDg`) by the YouTube creator eVRydayVR.

Setting the mood

Establishing the correct mood and setting is the first step in crafting a zombie-themed movie. Fear, dread, and isolation are a few tools used to establish fear in the audience, which is a good reason to use these tools in our scene.

We'll start by creating a new skybox. This skybox will be used to establish a sense of dread and foreboding in our game. With a darkened sky, the approaching zombies will *appear* out of the gloom adding to the fear and isolation of the scene:

1. Create a new material and rename it `Dark Sky`. Change the shader in the **Inspector** to **Shader: Skybox/Cubemap**. The shader setting is the first option in the **Inspector** as shown in *Figure 6.3*:

Figure 6.3: Setting the Shader for the new material

2. Set the **Tint Color** to Black or near Black. Try using `#0B0B0B00` as a starting point.
3. Select the **Lighting** tab to expose the environmental settings. Set the **Skybox Material** to the new **Dark Sky** material.
4. Scroll down to **Mixed Lighting** and uncheck **Baked Global Illumination**.
5. Scroll down further to **Other Settings** and check the **Fog option**.
6. Set the color to the same value used for the Dark Sky Tint Color and set the **Mode** to **Exponential** and set the **Density** to meet your needs. Start with `0.14` and adjust as needed.

> The Fog effect overlays a color onto objects in a scene. The density/opacity of the overlay is based on the object's distance from the camera. Learn more about this post-processing in the online documentation at: `https://docs.unity3d.com/Manual/PostProcessing-Fog.html`.

7. If you haven't done so already, deactivate the `Production Lighting` GameObject.
8. Play the game to test the mood. After testing, adjust the flashlight or skybox as appropriate.

Building an executable

Creating an executable does not require any special settings. The process is similar to creating any other standalone application:

1. Select **Build Settings** from the **File** menu.
2. Confirm that `ShootingRange` is in the Scenes in Build box. If it is not, simply click the **Add Open Scene** button.
3. Set the **Platform** to PC, Mac, Linux Standalone.
4. Click the **Build** button. A dialog will ask where to save your application. It is standard practice to create a `Builds` folder at the top level of the `Project` directory. Do so now, or save the application to another location.
5. Once the application is complete, quit Unity and launch the application.

Summary

We introduced several techniques and procedures for using Physic Raycasters to implement gaze interaction. The Unity manual and YouTube provide even deeper instruction in these areas through text and video tutorials.

Gaze input is only one of many ways to implement interaction in VR. Although we've mentioned this several times, the Unity VR Interaction tutorial is a treasure trove of information on this subject. Be sure to visit: `https://unity3d.com/learn/tutorials/topics/virtual-reality/interaction-vr`, before you start planning and building your own interactive VR experiences.

Our exploration of this project is complete, but your continuous learning has just begun. Start by visiting the **Asset Store** and downloading additional asset packages that might fit our environment.

Following are a few packages to add spice to the alleyway:

- Street Alley Pack- 34 models: `http://u3d.as/1CW`
- Urban City Series: `http://u3d.as/9Bp`
- Modular City Alley Pack: `http://u3d.as/w0i`

Figure 6.4: Assets from the Modular City Alley Pack

Expanding the experience

And don't stop at just cosmetics; consider other features that could improve the player's experience in your VR world. Here are a few challenges to consider:

- Try adding additional spawning locations or randomizing the current locations so that they change on each game start.
- The `Zombies` currently move at a standard speed. Try increasing the `ZombieController` base **Move Speed** by `0.25` after a zombie is killed. This will add a bit of a challenge for your players.
- Use a UI Canvas to implement a health/damage system. Give the player three lives and keep track of how many zombies are returned to the grave.
- Add environmental sounds to heighten the suspense.
- Add a weapon to help the player visualize the experience. Try adding the PM-40 (`http://u3d.as/mK7`) to the `CenterEyeAnchor`.

Carnival Midway Games — Part 1

7

"After 37 years of making games, I only now feel like I found my groove. No one starts day one and says 'Hey, I am a master at this.' Be intimidated. Experiment. Make something good or bad but make it. I am still far from mastering anything. And that's okay."

- Brenda Romero, Game Designer

This project will be the capstone in our exploration of virtual reality. So far, we have evaluated stationary scenes where the player has limited interaction with the environment. But now we will focus on three additional types of interaction: navigation, grasping, and tracking.

This final project is a carnival scene with two midway-style games to illustrate interactivity. By completing this project, you will be able to craft immersive experiences for entertainment and educational applications. Yes, these exercises are used to create thrilling VR game titles, but they can also be used to train new factory employees, help users overcome social anxiety, or explore the presentation of data in a whole new way. We urge you to think beyond the task at hand and instead consider the broader possibilities presented by virtual reality.

Recreating carnival games

The technology company, NVIDIA, has built a VR demo called VR Funhouse which runs on both the Oculus Rift and the HTC Vive. The game uses the precise gestures and movement of VR controllers to simulate games commonly found at carnival midways. For our project, we'll recreate two common games: Whack-a-Mole and Milk Bottle Toss:

Figure 7.1: Carnival scene photograph for inspiration

Preproduction

We've all visited a carnival. The festive atmosphere is community oriented with a general sense of awe and wonderment. The midway is a section where people play games, compete for prizes, and eat foods that we know aren't good for us, but we indulge nonetheless. NVIDIA's VR Funhouse doesn't have food, but it is a collection of seven mini games. The player accesses each game from the controller and interaction involves shooting arrows, slashing with a sword, swinging mallets, tossing basketballs, and shooting paint-filled silly guns.

For our project, we are going to create something a little different. Instead of reloading the world to start another game, our players will traverse the virtual space, taking small steps or *teleporting*, to access the play areas confined within the carnival environment. In this manner, we will be able to discuss mobility along with design, scripting, testing, and deployment on the Rift platform.

As part of the preproduction phase, we have taken the liberty of outlining the midway concept. We reviewed various carnival layouts and chose a design which should meet our needs. *Figure 7.2* includes a sketch of three design options. We chose Option C, which puts our game booths in a semi circle allowing for freedom of movement and a line of sight to each game. This was our approach, but more than for any of the other projects in this book, we urge you to experiment with your own layouts and use our idea as a starting point for your own work:

Figure 7.2: Layout ideas

Special production note

Before we begin, it is worth noting one of the challenges for writing this book. Like most development tools, Unity is constantly evolving as the developers make improvements and extend its functionality. These projects have been tested with three versions of Unity and two versions of the OVRPlugin for compatibility and accuracy. Our goal was to provide instructions which cover a wide range of user setups. But even with the extensive testing, we were often plagued by the speed at which Oculus and Unity made changes to their products. It is extremely difficult to stay on the cutting edge of ever-evolving platforms, technologies, and methodologies.

Where possible, we've included alternate instructions for a few procedures, but readers should visit `https://unity3d.com/unity/roadmap`, to keep up to date with features and functionality of the engine.

Requirements

You'll need the following to complete this assignment:

- An Oculus Rift and experience of exploring virtual reality games and applications.
- A control device (Oculus Remote or Touch Controller).
- A computer system which meets the required specification. Visit the Oculus Support page at `https://support.oculus.com/rift/`, to make sure your computer meets the system requirements.
- An installed version of Unity 5.6.x, or 2017.2+.

Although we will walk step-by-step through the development process, it is also advisable that the reader is familiar with some of the best practices for developing VR applications. These best practices can be found at `https://developer3.oculus.com/documentation/intro-vr/latest/`.

Process overview – Part 1

Because of the size and scope of the tasks associated with this project, we will break down the content into two parts. Part 1, listed as follows, addresses the early stages of development. These include setting up the software environment, constructing the gameplay environment, and implementing the macro-navigational system:

- Preparing Unity for VR development on the Rift
- Loading the **Oculus Virtual Reality Plugin (OVRP)**
- Building the game environment
- Combating motion sickness
- Implementing movement

Preparing Unity for VR development on the Rift

We will be using the free Unity Personal License for Unity 2017.3 which, along with Unity 5.x, offers built-in support for the Rift. You are free to use any license available from the Unity site. Additionally, it is not required to have a Rift installed to build a VR application, but having the device installed on the same computer will shorten the development time greatly.

 If you are just setting up your Rift computer, visit Unity's *Preparing for Rift Development* page for detailed instructions on preparing for Oculus development: `https://developer.oculus.com/documentation/unity/latest/concepts/unity-pcprep/`.

With the software installed, we can begin by creating a new Unity project. By default, Unity will store new projects in the same location as the previous project. For my work, I generally create a single directory for Unity projects and sub-directories for organization:

1. Launch Unity 2017.3 and create a new project. I've named the project `Midway` and stored it with the other projects:

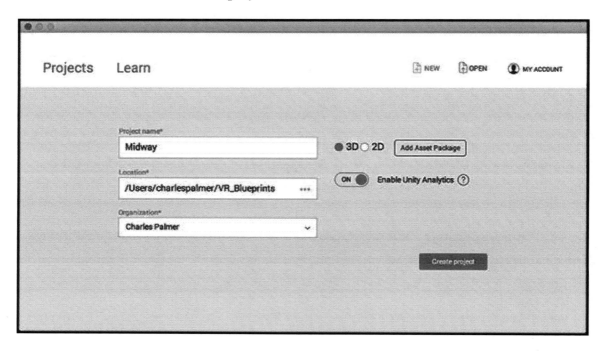

Figure 7.3: New project window

2. Choose **File | Build Settings...** and set the platform to PC, Mac, Linux, and Standalone. You'll also need to click the **Switch Platform** button if you need to make a change.
3. Choose **Player Settings...** from the button or the **Edit | Project Settings | Player** menu.
This will display the **PlayerSetting** window in the **Inspector**.
4. The **Inspector** panel will open displaying the PC, Mac, Linux, and Standalone settings. If these settings are not visible, return to the **Build Settings** window and confirm this choice.

5. Turn on Virtual Reality Support under the **XR Settings** at the bottom of the **Inspector** window. For Unity 5.5 through 2017.1.2, this setting can be found in the section labeled **Other Settings**.
6. Add the Oculus SDK if it is not present in the list.
7. Close the **Build Settings** window.

Unity is now ready to create a VR experience. Before hitting the Play button, make sure the Oculus application is running in the background. This is the same application used to launch games and search the Oculus Store. Then run the scene by hitting the Play button. Our scene will load in the **Game** window and the Rift headset. But since we haven't added any GameObjects, the experience will be very boring.

Although the main camera works during this test, it will not be used during production. Instead we will use the OVRCameraRig, which comes with a host of assets, scripts, and functionalities.

Loading the OVRP

The Oculus Integration package contains the tools, prefabs, samples, and scripts needed to develop VR applications. The package also includes the latest version of the OVRPlugin. This plugin is already part of the Unity editor, but upgrading to the latest version assures that we have access to the must current revisions, scripts, and assets. In the next step, we will import the OVRPlugin package:

1. Open the **Asset Store** (*Ctrl + 9* on Windows or *Cmd + 9* on Mac) and search for Oculus Integration. It will be the first search result.
2. Click the package link and choose **Import**.

   The Import dialog will display the package's components. This is everything we need to build our VR experience. Confirm that everything is selected before proceeding.

3. With everything selected, click the **Import** button in the lower right-hand corner. Depending on your platform, version, and past VR projects, you might see two or three dialog boxes regarding out-of-date scripts or plugins. Click the affirmative Yes or Okay to continue, and choose **Restart** if asked.
4. Go make a sandwich or do something fun. The process of importing involves compiling shaders for your graphics card. The actual time varies depending on the operation system and video card. But times from 5 - 25 minutes have been reported.

When completed, the `Asset` directory will look like the following image. These added directories contain scripts for VR camera behavior, prefabs, input API for controllers, advanced rendering features, object-grabbing, and haptics scripts for Touch, as well as debugging tools. Most of these things work in the background, but we will be using the prefabs to build our scene:

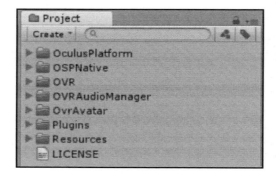

Figure 7.4: Asset folder after importing the Oculus Integration package

Setting up the project

With the Oculus VR packages installed, we will now focus on the environment. This step will involve constructing a scene where the gameplay will take place. But we will approach it a little differently from previous projects. Instead of a step-by-step guide, we will work with building a few modular set pieces which you can arrange to create your custom midway:

1. Use **Assets** | **Create** | **Folder** to create the following folders; `Animations`, `Audio`, `Fonts`, `Materials`, `Prefabs`, `Scenes`, and `Scripts`. As various asset types are created, we will move them to the proper folder to keep the `Asset` directory organized.

2. Select **File** | **Save As...** to save the current scene as `Main.unity` into the `Assets/Scenes` folder.

3. Select the **Directional Light** in the **Hierarchy** panel. Set the **Shadow Type** to **Soft Shadows** and the **Realtime Shadows Strength** to `0.4` in the **Inspector** panel.

4. Set the **Draw Mode** to **Shaded Wireframe** in the **Scene** view menu bar. This is a cosmetic setting that will help align and identify various objects in the scene. *Figure 7.5* shows the options location in the menu bar.

5. Delete the scene's `Main Camera` GameObject. Doing this will display the Display 1 No cameras rendering warning in the **Game** window. This is normal. We will be adding a new camera in the next section:

Figure 7.5: Setting the Draw Mode in the Scene view bar to improve object identification

Creating the player avatar

Virtual reality applications provide a first-person view for the player. Because interaction is so important, Oculus also provides tools for visualizing the user's hands and the torsos of other players in multiplayer or social media titles. In these steps, we will add the `OVRPlayerController` prefab. This item contains a camera, tracking tools, and scripts for managing interactions:

1. Locate the `OVRPlayerController` in the **Project** window under `OVR | Prefabs`. Drag this prefab into the **Hierarchy** window and set its position to (0, 1.8, -8).

2. Expose the `OVRPlayerController` to reveal the `OVRCameraRig/TrackingSpace`. Drag the `LocalAvatar` from `OvrAvatar/Content/Prefabs` into `TrackingSpace`.

3. Select the `LocalAvatar` GameObject and make sure the **Start With Controller** checkbox under **Ovr Avatar (Script)** is unchecked.

4. Add a 3D plane to the scene. Rename the plane `Ground`, set its **Position** to (0, 0, -6) and the **Scale** to (2.5, 1, 2).

5. Save the scene.

6. Hit play.

Although our scene is still blank, we now have hands in our scene. The fingers are mapped to buttons on the Touch controllers, so touching certain buttons will make the hands point, grasp, and relax:

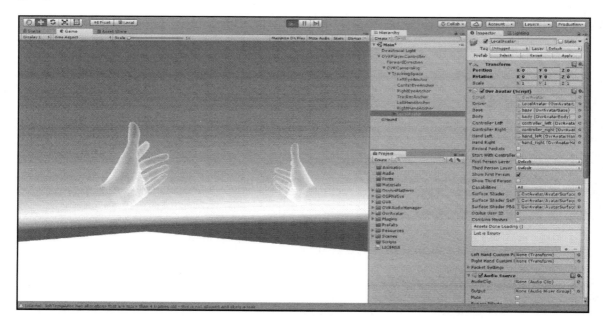

Figure 7.6: Game window at runtime with controller hands

Designing the play area

As mentioned, we'll use a modular approach for building the environment geometry. We'll need assets such as the gameplay booths, various background elements, interactive items, and other components, as needed, to build the mood. But instead of fully visualizing each asset, we will use a level design technique for blocking out the design.

Gray boxing (also known as blue boxing, white boxing, blocking out, or blocking in) is a game development term used to describe an early layout phase of level design. Designers use standard modeling primitives (cubes, planes, columns, spheres...) to create rough layouts of gameplay areas. Environmental details are limited; there are no textures, rough shapes, and flat lighting, just gray shapes used as placeholders to help designers reference scale, identify navigational pathways, look for choke points, demonstrate physics functionality, and test object colliders.

This approach allows for quick iteration because layouts can be implemented and tested by one person in a few minutes, rather than days. The term *gray box* comes from the primitive object's lack of color, textures, or materials.

In October 2017, a few level designers at Naughty Dog started the hashtag `#blocktober`. It quickly caught on and designers from across the world started revealing a part of the design process seldom seen outside of development studios. A few examples from Twitter are shown in *Figure 7.7*. But this is only the tip of the iceberg. We urge you to search the `#blocktober` and find some examples of your own:

Figure 7.7: Examples from #blocktober 2017

For our Midway project, we will take a similar approach and gray-box the scene. Instead of fleshing out the complete GameObject details, simple Unity primitives with basic gray materials will be used to demonstrate how users play with the carnival games:

1. Create three materials called `BackgroundGrey`, `ForegroundGrey`, and `InteractiveGrey`. Set their colors to dark gray for the background, a medium gray for the foreground, and a lighter gray for the interactive material. These will be used to help identify various GameObjects and focus our design efforts.

2. Move the new materials to the `Materials` folder.

Building the game environment

Before we begin construction, we will set up the snap values. GameObjects can be constrained to move, scale, or rotate according to the snap setting. This is a very useful technique for setting the relative positions of objects.

When positioning objects we'll use one of three techniques:

- **Grid snapping (Control-drag)**: This method will transform the object using the snap settings. These values are set in the **Snap Setting...** dialog.
- **Vertex snapping (v-drag)**: This method snaps the currently selected vertex to a vertex on a second object. Hitting the *V* key will turn on the closest vertex.
- **Surface snapping (Control-Shift-drag)**: This method will be your best friend. After selecting an object, this keystroke will display a square gizmo at the object's center. Grabbing this widget will snap the object to a surface on the nearest GameObject.

Using the Snap settings is a time-saver for constructing the gameplay environment. It speeds up the building process by making it easier to align objects in 3D space. Follow these steps to setup snapping and start the construction process:

1. Choose **Edit | Snap Settings...** from the application menu. The *Snap* feature will let us *snap* the transform settings to predetermined increments:

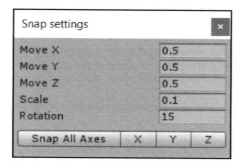

Figure 7.8: Set the Snap settings before constructing GameObjects

2. Create an empty GameObject at the root level of the **Hierarchy** panel. Rename the GameObject to Environment and position it at (0,0,0). We will use it to house the environmental assets.

3. Move the Ground asset we created earlier into the Environment GameObject and set its material to BackgroundGrey.

4. Save the scene.

Building the game booth

Next, we will construct the generic *hut* which will be used to house each of the midway booths. This quick mock-up would be replaced during the refinement phase, but for now we just need a shape which sets the scale for each midway game:

1. Create another empty GameObject at the root level, rename it Booth, and set its position to (0,0,0).

2. Create eight cubes as children of the Booth GameObject and transform them using the following settings:

	Position	Rotate	Scale
WallBack	0, 1, 1.5	0, 0, 0	4, 2.4, 0.05
WallLeft	-2, 1, 0.5	0, 90, 0	2, 2.4, 0.05
WallRight	2, 1, 0.5	0, 90, 0	2, 2.4, 0.05
Roof	0, 2.4, 0	90, 0, 0	4.1, 3, 0.05
ColumnLeft	-2, 1, -1.4	0, 0, 0	0.1, 2.4, 0.1
ColumnRight	2, 1, -1.4	0, 0, 0	0.1, 2.4, 0.1
Counter	0, 0.9, -1.5	0, 0, 0	4, 0.05, 0.5
Kickboard	0, 0.45, -1.4	0, 0, 0	4.0, 0.9, 0.1
Sign	0, 2.5, -1.55	80, 0, 0	4.2, 0.02, 0.9

Table 7.1: GameObjects used to construct the booth

3. Set the material for each cube to ForegroundGrey.

4. Save the scene.

Adding 3D text

In Unity, text can be created as 2D sprites or 3D GameObjects. 2D sprites are used as user-interface elements. They are added to canvases and display as an overlay on the user's view of the scene. 3D text elements are used as a GameObject with the same transforms, components, and attributes as other scene items. For this project, we will use 3D text GameObjects to give the booths a name:

1. Visit a free font repository, such as 1001freefonts.com or Fontspring.com, to locate and download a font of your liking. Select a font that is either TrueType (.ttf files) or OpenType (.otf files) for the best results.

2. Add the font to the project by right-clicking in the **Project** window and selecting **Import New Asset...** and move it into the Font folder.

3. Select the font and change its **Font Size** to 90 in the **Inspector**.

By default, imported font assets will have their font size set to 16 points. This is not the size used to present the font in the scene. Instead, this size is used by the render engine to create the text mesh. Without this change, the text may appear blocky and blurry when used in a GameObject.

Figure 7.9 shows a comparison of two 3D text GameObjects using the Arcon font type. The left asset has the default **Font Size** 16 and a default **Character Size** of 1. The right GameObject uses adjusted values. The font asset has a **Font Size** of 90 while the **Character Size** is set at 0.17. The result produces a sharp, crisp GameObject:

Figure 7.9: Setting the Font Size of imported font assets will result in sharper 3D text elements

The following steps outline the process for adding 3D Text objects to the scene. These objects will be used on the signs above each game booth:

1. Right-click the `Sign` GameObject and choose **3D Object** | **3D Text**. This will create a 3D text element as a child to the `Sign` object.

2. In the **Inspector** panel, change the following components:
   - GameObject name = `BoothName`
   - Transform
   - **Position**: (0, 2.5, -1.55)
   - **Rotation**: (-10, 0, 0)
   - **Size**: (0.6, 0.6, 0.6)

- **Text Mesh**
- **Text:** `Booth Title - This is placeholder text`
- **Character Size** = `0.1`
- **Anchor** = **Middle Center**
- **Alignment** = **Center**
- **Font** = *set to your font asset*

3. Make any additional adjustments to the GameObject to fit your scene.

Creating the booth prefab

Our booth is now complete. We will need three copies of the completed object. But instead of using duplicate, we will turn the object into a prefab. The Unity prefab asset type is a convenient method for creating asset templates. An instance of a prefab contains the components, properties, and values from the original and changes can easily be applied to all instances. Prefab creation is simple, and should be used whenever multiple copies of an object are needed:

1. Drag the `Booth` GameObject to the `Project/Prefabs` folder. This process will create a template asset which will be used to populate the scene with additional game booths:

Figure 7.10: Prefab items have a cube icon in the Project window and will be displayed with blue text in the Hierarchy window

2. Save the scene before continuing. *Figure 7.11* represents our work so far:

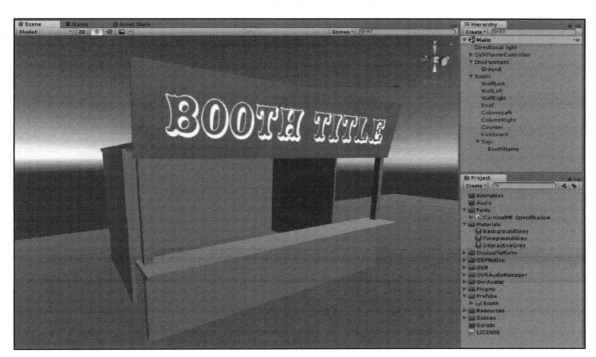

Figure 7.11: Booth construction

Planning the midway activities

Our midway will have three booths. Two will contain activities that we create in this tutorial, while the third will be left for you to design your own game. All three will use the general booth prefabs with slight modifications:

1. Drag two more booth prefabs into the scene.
2. Rename the booths BottleSmash, WackyMoles, and Closed.
3. Navigate to **Hierarchy** | **BottleSmash** | **sign** and select the BoothTitle GameObject.
4. In the **Inspector** window, change the **Text** value in the Text Mesh component to Milk Bottle Toss.

5. Adjust the **Character Size** as needed. The booth in your scene should now reflect the activity we will create in the next chapter.

6. Repeat this for the other two booths.

7. Relocate the booths to be side-by-side or in a slight arc to make it easy for our player to move between games. For our example, we left the `WackyMoles` booth at the origin (0, 0, 0) and repositioned the other two, as shown in *Figure 7.12*.

These booths will be the focus of our activities. We'll use lighting, color, scale, and object placement to attract the players to this area.

Adding clutter to the scene

Clutter is generally a bad thing. But in game development, clutter is the addition of scene elements which help make the space *feel* real. Think back to your last time visiting a carnival or street fair. What elements, other than the game booths, brought the experience to life? Was it vendor stalls, exotic food trucks, mechanical rides, or live animals? Was it the city street, state fairgrounds, or big top that defined the environment? Use your imagination and decide what the scene needs to be complete. But remember, we are still at the gray box stage, so keep the details to a minimum. Use empty GameObjects and folders to keep the **Hierarchy** and **Project** windows organized:

- Research carnival imagery
- Add primitive game objects to flesh out the scene
- Save the scene and the project

Figure 7.12 is a sample of how your environment might look as clutter; the secondary items are added to the scene. In our scene, we found a few trees and fences in the Asset Store, before creating the ferris wheel, trash cans, crates, and entrance sign:

 Unity has a built-in, simple-to-use editor for designing trees. Visit the Tree Editor documentation to learn more about this powerful tool and how to add trees to your projects: `https://docs.unity3d.com/Manual/class-Tree.html`.

Figure 7.12: Sample of the midway environment

Combating VR sickness

Kinetosis, or motion sickness, is caused when there is a disconnect between our visual system and vestibular system. It's when our eyes detect movement that is not sensed by our inner ear. The conflict makes our brain think we have been poisoned and begins sending signals to our body to flush a none existent toxin. The result will vary according to user sensitivity, but it often causes discomfort, nausea, profuse sweating, dizziness, headaches, vertigo, excessive salivating, or all of these things. Since the late 1950s, the digital version of motion sickness, simulation sickness, has been greatly researched and documented by the US Military in relation to the development of training simulators. Today, these same factors are true for many computer game players with the effects seemingly magnified by VR experiences.

A slight semantic difference:
Motion sickness is caused by a disconnect between two physically moving objects; think of a passenger on a boat. Simulation sickness is caused by the perceived disconnect between a user and the digital environment.

Anyone can develop simulation sickness and since we have yet to have a definitive technical solution, it is the developer's responsibility to manage and mitigate the issue. The following sub sections present six techniques for reducing the effects of simulation sickness.

Eliminating non-forward motion

Movement is the biggest cause of simulation sickness, especially movement that is counter to how we behave in the real world. Non-forward motion is very common in computer games where the player can move in one direction while looking in another. Eliminating this type of movement may not be possible in all situations, but it should at least be reduced. One suggestion would be to reduce the player's speed greatly when looking in a direction that is greater than 15-25° of their movement vector.

Consider adding UI overlays

For me, overlays or static portions of the viewing area greatly reduce simulation sickness. Adding an overlay won't work in all situations, but keep in mind that creating areas of the screen which ground the player's perception of the world, will help many users.

Figure 7.13 is a collection of examples which immerse the player in VR experiences while reducing simulation sickness. The images are, clockwise from the upper left:

- The cockpit environment in *EVE: Valkyrie*
- The helmet visor in *Valiant*
- Persistent interface elements in *Time Rifters*
- An example from researchers at *Purdue University*

Where they've seen a 13.5% reduction in simulation sickness by adding a fake nose to the experience:

Figure 7.13: UI overlays

Reducing acceleration

The vestibular system, which controls our balance, is very sensitive to accelerations. Changes in velocity and angular motion increase the potential for making people sick. If a vehicular move is required, try keeping the movement at a constant velocity and limit the number of curves and jumps.

Reducing yaw

Yaw is motion (typically in a vehicle) around the vertical axis, turning left or right. In VR applications, this movement is typically controlled by the user's head. But in some cases, designers have translated control of the yaw to an analog stick, keyboard, or other controller input. This is one of the quickest ways to make your user sick. If 360° freedom is needed, we often have the user stand or sit in a swivel chair.

Reducing vection

When a large portion of the viewer's field of vision moves, the viewer *feels* like they have moved. This illusion of motion is called *vection* and it can also lead to motion sickness.

Using appropriate motions

The player should be in control of all motion. Features such as head bob, slow motion, and axis rotation (twisting cameras) are jarring and increase discomfort for the player. If needed, they must be used sparingly and in short durations.

In *Spider-Man Homecoming Virtual Reality Experience*, CreateVR used a mixture of overlay and limited motion to recreate the hero's signature web-swinging move. Players select the anchor target and fire a web strand. Motion control then switches to a system where a roughly 3-second swinging sequence, complete with focus overlay, carries the player to their destination:

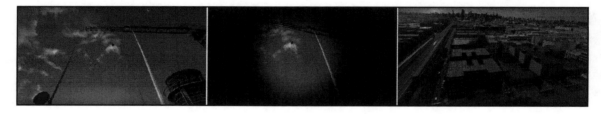

Figure 7.14: Mixing overlay and motion to ease player discomfort

This topic has been widely discussed in depth across the media landscape. To learn more, check out a few of these links:

- Designing to Minimize Simulation Sickness in VR Games *(highly recommended)*:
  https://www.youtube.com/watch?v=2UF-7BVf1zs
- VR Camera Movements Techniques:
  https://uploadvr.com/introducing-limbo-a-vr-camera-movement-technique-by-the-developers-of-colosse/
- Simulator Sickness in Virtual Environments:
  http://oai.dtic.mil/oai/oai?verb=getRecord&metadataPrefix=html&identifier=ADA295861
- 11 Ways to Prevent Motion Sickness!:
  http://riftinfo.com/oculus-rift-motion-sickness-11-techniques-to-prevent-it

Next we will focus on constructing comfortable experiences for VR users.

Implementing movement

Our final application will permit micro-navigation via physical movement. These movements are captured by the Rift's sensors and touch controllers to detect walking, grasping, and swinging. But at approximately 21 m², our environment is much larger than a typical 3.9 m² Rift setup space. This means that we need a different system to facilitate macro-navigations.

As noted in the previous section, the need for large-scale movement is a general source of unease in virtual environments. We need a solution which uses forward motion, has reduced or no acceleration, does not support head swivel, and provides a feeling of control for the player. One simple way to achieve these requirements is gaze-based teleportation.

A gaze-based teleportation system

In gaze-based teleportation, the player focuses on a location, the system provides visual feedback, the player responds with controller input (a gesture or button-click), and teleportation occurs with or without transitional effects. For our midway, we will provide a GameObject to indicate player gaze and provide a destination for the teleportation. This object will only be displayed when the player gazes at ground-level teleportation locations, indicating a wish to travel to that location. We will then map the primary controller button to trigger positional transformation of the `LocalAvatar` GameObject. Remember this GameObject contains the POV camera, controller hands, and the player's colliders. To the user, it will appear as if they have been teleported to a new location, retaining their previous head and tilt positional values:

1. Create an empty root-level GameObject, rename it `TeleportSystem`, and set the Position Transform to (0, 0, -4). The GameObject will contain the player's macro-navigation assets.
2. Add a cube to `TeleportSystem` positioned at (0, 0, 0.66) with a scale of (3.8, 0.01, 3.5). Rename the cube `TeleportArea (1)`.

The `TeleportArea` GameObject will be used to indicate areas accessible by the player. Once the other assets are prepared, we will duplicate the `TeleportAreas` to fit the space:

1. Create a new layer called `TeleportTrigger`.
2. Assign `TeleportArea (1)` to the `TeleportTrigger`.
3. Add a cylinder to `TeleportSystem` positioned at (0, 0.005, 0) with a scale of (1, 0.0025, 1).

4. Rename the cylinder `TeleportTarget` and set **Is Trigger** to true for the capsule collider.

5. Create a new C# script called `Teleporter` and put it in the `Script` folder.

6. Assign the script to the `LocalAvatar` GameObject.

7. Double-click the `Teleporter` script to open the editor.

The `Teleporter` script is broken into a few distinct sections. Perform the following steps to create the required behaviors.

8. Add the `teleporter` and `layerMask` variables:

```
using System.Collections;
using System.Collections.Generic;
using UnityEngine;

public class Teleporter : MonoBehaviour {
    [SerializeField] GameObject target;
    [SerializeField] LayerMask layerMask;
```

9. Delete the `Start()` function and add the following to `Update()`:

```
void Update () {
    RaycastHit hit;
    if (Physics.Raycast (Camera.main.transform.position,
    Camera.main.transform.rotation *
    Vector3.forward, out hit, 9999, layerMask)) {
        target.SetActive (true);
        target.transform.position = hit.point;
    } else {
        target.SetActive (false);
    }
    if (Input.GetButtonDown("Button.One") ||
        Input.GetButtonDown("Button.Three")) {
        Vector3 markerPosition = target.transform.position;
        transform.position = new Vector3 (markerPosition.x,
        transform.position.y, markerPosition.z);
    }
}
}
```

The `Update()` function first creates a `RaycastHit` called a hit and then tests if the ray has collided with an object on the `layerMask` layer. If a hit is registered, then the visible target is turned on and moved to the point where the ray passes through the `layerMask`. This statement also hides the target if a hit is not registered.

The second `if` statement checks to see if a specific button on the right (`Button.One`) or left (`Button.Three`) controller was pressed. (See *Figure 7.15* for a mapping of the controller buttons.) If a press was detected, then the position of the target is stored, and the player's transform position is set to the same location. This results in the actual teleportation, because we move the player to a new location, instantly changing their point of view in the scene:

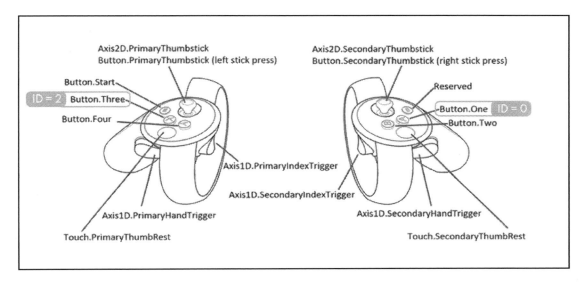

Figure 7.15: Touch controller button mapping

Mapping touch controller buttons

Although we used the *X* and *A* buttons, feel free to use whichever button combination works for your situation. The Unity documentation has a complete mapping for the Oculus, Gear VR and Vive controllers at
`https://docs.unity3d.com/Manual/OculusControllers.html`. The mapping contains the name, interaction type, and ID of each button. These values are needed to tell Unity how to handle button inputs.

Depending on your version of the OVRPlugin or Unity, the `Teleporter` script may not work as expected. You may also have to add input settings for the controller buttons. Perform the following steps below to map the controller inputs:

1. Select **Edit | Project Settings | Input** from the main menu.
2. The **Inspector** panel now displays the button mapping for Unity. If the list is empty, try clicking on the **Axes** title to expose the option.
3. If `Button.One` is not present, duplicate one of the existing entries and change the values to match those in *Figure 7.16*. Be sure to match the text exactly; include capitalization, spacing, and drop-down values:

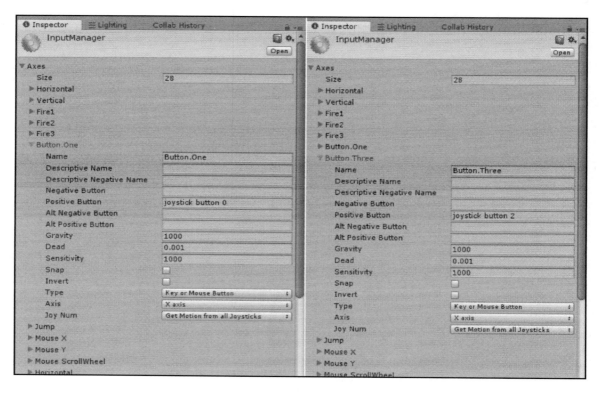

Figure 7.16: Adding array elements for Button.One and Button.Three

4. Select the `LocalAvatar` GameObject.

5. The script required two variables. Drag the `TeleportTarget` GameObject to the target variable. Set the layer mask to `TeleportTrigger`.

6. Before testing the script, move the `Tracking` to **Position** (0, 1.8, −6) **Rotation** (0, 0, 0).

If we tried to play the scene right now, everything would work, except that the teleporter would teleport us below the `TeleportArea` GameObject. This is because our `OVRCameraRig` is tracking the player's position based on the camera's eye level. We can correct this issue, by changing the tracking type:

1. Select the `OVRCameraRig` GameObject and view the **OVR Manager (Script)** component. Under the Tracking heading there is an attribute for **Tracking Origin Type**. Change this value to **Floor Level**.

2. Play the scene.

   The teleportation target should follow your gaze as you look at the `TeleportArea (1)` GameObject. And when it is visible, clicking the *X* or *A* button will teleport you to that location. Expand the teleport range by duplicating and increasing the `TeleportArea (1)` GameObject.

3. Create two or three duplicates of the `TeleportArea (1)` GameObject. Arrange two of the objects to provide access to the `Wacky Mole` and `Bottle Smash` booths. But you can also add others to let the player move about the scene. *Figure 7.17* shows a simple layout of the GameObjects. Use the following list when considering teleport locations:
   - Choose locations that provide areas of interest to the player.
   - Keep teleport areas at ground-level.
   - Avoid overlaying any of the teleport areas. In some instances, this causes flickering and visual artifacting across the scene.
   - There is considerable scientific debate on what happens when atoms are instantaneously teleported into the same space. The leading theory is that the overlap of electron clouds would produce a very large and potentially messy, nuclear explosion. So just to be safe, avoid teleporting players into any solid objects.

4. Deactivate the Mesh Renderer for each of the `TeleportArea (x)` objects. This will hide the objects from sight, but the object's collider will still be available for the Physics Raycaster generated by the `Teleporter` script.

5. Save the project and scene:

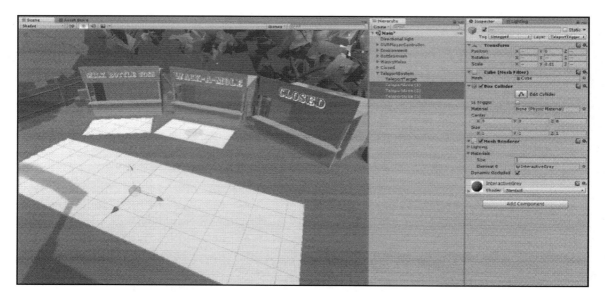

Figure 7.17: TeleportArea GameObjects are added to provide access to various parts of the scene

Deactivating stick movement [Optional]

The `OVRPlayerController` prefab includes the `OVRPlayerController` script. This script does many things right, but it also facilitates stick movement. Stick movement uses the touch controller's analog sticks for directional movement and rotation. During development, it provides a quick means to move around the scene while in VR. But in practice, it induces motion sickness for the following reasons:

- It introduces non-forward motion
- It increases vection
- It moves yaw control to the touch controller

We generally eliminate stick movement, or at least expose the feature in the Inspector so it can be controlled. The following steps are optional, but highly recommended for player comfort:

1. Locate the `OVRPlayerController` script in the **Project** window. In version 1.21.0, the script can be found her **OVR | Scripts | Util**.
2. Open the script in a script editor.

   The script controls player movement in the `UpdateMovement ()` function. This function contains a series of `if` statements which control when and how movement should occur. In theory, we could go through and comment out several lines to achieve our goal of deactivating stick movement. But instead, we will simply take advantage of the existing formula used to compute the move distance.

3. Locate the private float `SimulationRate` and set its value to zero. Since this variable is used to compute the linear distance of movement from the controller, setting its value to zero will stop all stick movement. Unfortunately, the variable is also used to compute the speed at which gravity affects the player during freefall. To fix this, we will create a new variable for falls.
4. On the following line, create a new float named `FallRate` and set its value to `60f`.
5. Change the variable `SimulationRate` to `FallRate` in the following statements:

```
(~Line 208)
 FallSpeed += ((Physics.gravity.y * (GravityModifier * 0.002f)) *
SimulationRate * Time.deltaTime);

(~Line 210)
 moveDirection.y += FallSpeed * SimulationRate * Time.deltaTime;
```

Making objects grabbable

Our carnival midway is progressing nicely and with a teleporting function in place, the scene is becoming a fulfilling VR experience. In this next step, we will build the functions that make it possible to pick up and swing the matter for the *Wacky Moles* game and throw softballs in the *Milk Bottle Toss* game. If you have experience with the `OVRGrabber` and `OVRGrabble` scripts, feel free to implement the function and move on to the next section.

Follow along if this is your first time using these scripts:

1. Drill down to the `TrackingSpace` of the items in the `OVRPlayerController` prefab, as shown in *Figure 7.18*.

2. Right-click on the `LeftHandAnchor` and choose **3D Object | Sphere**. Rename the sphere `LeftGrabber` and set its scale to (`0.2, 0.2, 0.2`).

3. Complete this for the `RightHandAnchor` as well, naming the object `RightGrabber`. *Figure 7.18* shows the `LeftGrabber` and `RightGrabber` as being added to children of each anchor:

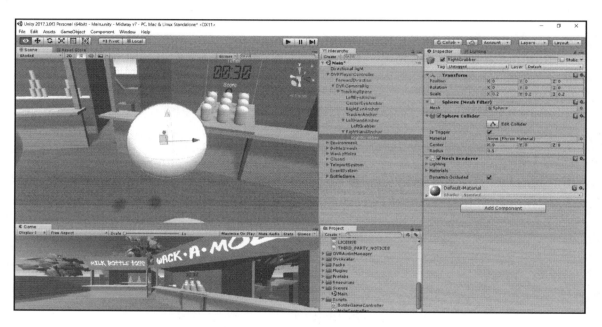

Figure 7.18: Creation of the LeftGrabber and RightGrabber used to facilitate grabbing objects

4. Hit Play and put on the headset.

The two spheres now snap into position and follow the hand movements of the touch controllers. Now that the objects are in place, we can add additional OVR scripts to the object anchors. Once the scripts are operational, the Mesh Renderer for the grabbers will be deactivated:

1. Drag the **OVR | Scripts | Util | OVRGrabber** script to the `LeftHandAnchor`.
2. The `LeftHandAnchor` will now have the `OVRGrabber` script and a Rigidbody component.
3. Select the Rigidbody component. Uncheck **Use Gravity** and check **Is Kinematic**. Without this step, our *hands* would drop to the ground plane instead of following our motion.
4. In the **OVR Grabber (Script)** component, change the **Grab Volume** size to 1.
5. Click the selection target for Grip Transform and select `LeftGrabber`. Remember that the `LeftGrabber` is where our hand is, so setting the object as the Grip Transform for the `LeftHandAchor` means that when we pick up an object, it will lock into the position of the `LeftGrabber` sphere.
6. Click the selection target for **Element 0** of the **Grab Volume** and select `LeftGrabber` again. This will use the `LeftGrabber` collider to determine if we can pick up an object.
7. Next, choose L Touch for the `Controller` value.
8. Select the `LeftGrabber` and change the Sphere Collider **Is Trigger** value to true by checking the checkbox.
9. Repeat steps 1-8 for the `RightHandAnchor` and `RightGrabber`.

The touch controllers can now pick up objects, but we must also define which objects can be grabbed. Since we have not created any game props, we will use a simple cube to test the function:

1. Add a cube to the scene, rename it `Block` and scale it down to $(0.2, 0.2, 0.2)$.
2. Add a Rigidbody component and drag the **OVR | Scripts | Util | OVRGrabbable** script to the `Block` GameObject.
3. Play the scene and grab the `Block`. You should be able to pick up the object, transfer it from hand to hand, and throw the block.

The last step is to replace the spheres with the avatar hands. To do this we will deactivate the Mesh Renderer of the spheres:

1. Select the `LeftGrabber` and `RightGrabber` and uncheck the Mesh Renderer component in the **Inspector** panel. This method works because we are only using the spherical collider for each grabber.
2. Save the scene and hit the Play button.

If all goes well, you should now have two hands instead of spheres in the scene. The hands will behave just like the spheres except that now the controllers will react to button presses, hovers, and trigger pulls.

Now that we understand how to make objects grabbable, we can implement this approach for using the mallet and softballs in our Midway games.

Summary

In the next chapter, we will construct the game props, animations, and scripts needed to facilitate gameplay in the scene. But for now, it might be a good time to add more environmental clutter. Are there objects or activities missing from our little scene? Use simple geometry and materials to flesh out the environment, limit the player's view, and keep focused on the midway booths.

Potential objects to include are the following:

- Smaller booths (ticket sales, fortune-tellers, a dunk tank, or a strongman game)
- Food vendors (cotton candy, hot dogs, deep-fried things on sticks...)
- Distant rides visible over fences and through trees
- Balloons attached to booths or other elements
- Random crates, barrels, and trash cans

8

Carnival Midway Games — Part 2

"Ideas are worthless until you get them out of your head to see what they can do."

- Unknown Hipster

The goal of Part 1 was to construct the overall environment. We built the play area and a teleportation system for navigating the space. Part 2 focuses on building the gameplay experience for each Midway game. This will include using primitive shapes to craft the props, building a state machine to control animation, and scripting the player and prop interactions. But before that, we should discuss a few different backup techniques.

Backing up the project

We have done a lot of work on this project. And according to Murphy's, Sod's, or Finagle's law, something bad is bound to happen at the worst possible moment. Computer crashes, corrupt files, lost data, and the like are inevitable in our computer-centric life. We can't avoid these things happening, but we can take precautions to mitigate the damage. The first step is to save often, while the second is to back up our work.

There are three primary types of backups we can create. Although the methods are generally related to your level of experience, we should always look for the method that is best for a given situation.

Local backup

This is the simplest method and ideal for novice users. The process is to create a duplicate (or zipped archive) of the entire Unity project folder. Some users report exporting the project game assets into a package as a solution for backups. While this is helpful for moving assets between projects, there are various project settings that are not retained within a new package.

Ideally, whichever local backup method you use, the resulting backup archive should be transferred to a separate drive for safe keeping.

Unity Collaborate

This is a cloud-hosted service used to share and synchronize work among small teams. But it is also a great way to save your project on a remote server. Once enabled, every change made within your project is logged and compared to a remote copy. Simply hit the **Publish Now** button when your local changes are ready to be synced with the remote project directory. For details on *Collaborate* and the other Unity Services, visit `https://unity3d.com/unity/features/collaborate`.

Software version control services

Version or source control is a method for organizing and tracking revisions within software development. Its strength comes from the ability to revert to previous revisions and support the work of multiple users. Details on implementing version control can be found in the *Version Control Integration* section of the Unity documentation: `https://docs.unity3d.com/Manual/Versioncontrolintegration.html`.

 Note: During development, a *No Oculus Rift App ID has been provided*. Warning may appear at the bottom of the **Game** window. A while an App ID is required to retrieve Oculus avatars for specific users, you can ignore this warning when constructing prototypes and test experiences.

Midway booth games

Just like their real-world equivalents, each of our games will take place in a separate booth. This will isolate the activities and get our player moving around the space. But before we can script the interactions, we need to build the game props. These props will be the interactive components of our scene, and each game requires a different set of props.

We will start with the Wacky Mole game and move on to the Milk Bottle Toss one, when it is complete. For the first game, we will need the following props:

- **Game table**: The structure where gameplay will take place
- **Moles**: Critters to be whacked
- **Score Board**: UI element for presenting the countdown clock and player score
- **Mallet**: A whacking device

Wacky Mole props

We need an empty GameObject to house the mole game itself. This base asset will contain the components needed to visualize the pop-up moles. But first we need to alter the scene, so we can focus on this new object without distraction:

1. Select the `Environment`, `BottleSmash`, `WackyMoles`, `Closed`, and `TeleportSystem` (everything but the lights and the `LocalAvatar`) GameObjects.
2. Uncheck the **Active** checkbox in the **Inspector** to hide the scene items.

Our scene is now blank, so we can work in isolation, around the origin point, without the worry of mistakenly modifying any of the environmental elements. We will use this space to construct the game components, sounds, scripts, and animation for the Wacky Mole game. Once built, we will move the primary GameObject to the correct position. *Figure 8.1* serves as a reference image.

We will refer to this image during construction:

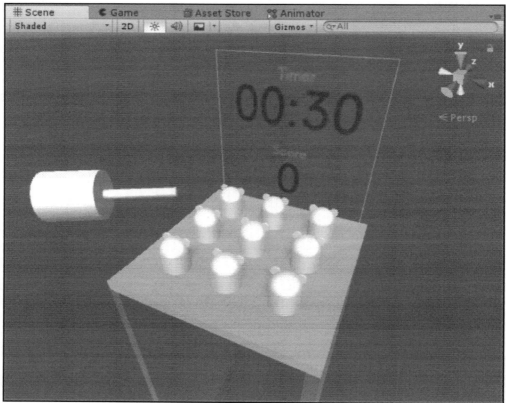

Figure 8.1: Reference image of the completed Mole Game prop

The GameTable

We will start by building the game's playing surface. This is a simple table top through which the moles will rise up. In our gray box environment, we have the luxury of using placeholders to determine the relative size, shape, and distances of environmental GameObjects. So instead of a table with nine holes, we'll use a simple cube:

1. Create an empty GameObject titled `MoleGame` and place it at (0, 0, 0). This will be our main container.

2. Create a second empty GameObject titled `GameTable` as a child of `MoleGame`.

3. Create a new cube at (0, 0, 0) called `Tabletop` as a child of `GameTable`.

4. Scale `Tabletop` to (`1.1, 0.06, 1.1`) and set the material to `ForegroundGrey`.

Remember this `GameTable` is only a placeholder. After testing the game's interaction and the player's engagement, the `GameTable` object would be replaced with a modeled asset containing holes for the moles to rise through. Currently, Unity does not have any native Boolean mesh modeling functions, but there are packages available that provide this function. If you wish to add and subtract mesh objects, search for **constructive solid geometry (CSG)** in the **Asset Store**:

1. Create two more cubes scaled to (`0.06, 2.4, 1.1`) within the `GameTable` GameObject.

2. Rename them `SideLeft` and `SideRight` and snap them to the sides of the `Tabletop` (see *Figure 8.2*). These pieces are optional, but when in place, they will help hide the underside of the game space.

3. Set the material for `SideRight` and `SideLeft` to `BackgroundGrey`.

4. Save the scene:

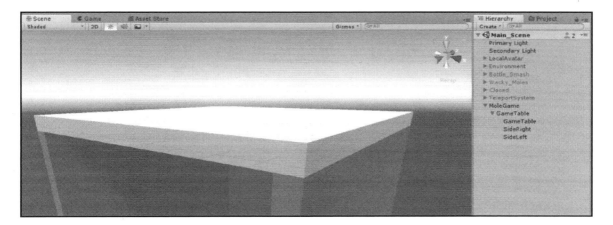

Figure 8.2: Detail of the GameTable with snapped corners

The mole

The Asset Store is full of mole assets starting at around US $ 4.00, but rather than pay for something, we will construct our own gray box asset. Our mole will be constructed of simple shapes and an animation. The mole will reside in an empty GameObject, which will serve as a container and positioning tool:

1. Create an empty GameObject as a child of `MoleGame` called `MolePosition (1)`. This item will contain our mole assets and be used to position the pesky varmint in the scene.

 We add `(1)` to the end of any GameObject that we plan to duplicate. When Unity duplicates the object, it will increment the number accordingly.

2. Create another empty GameObject. This one should be a child of `MolePosition (1)` called `Mole`.

With the containers in place, we can now begin constructing the mole.

3. Add a capsule to the `Mole` GameObject. Rename it `Body`, set the position to (0, 0.17, 0) and the scale to (0.2, 0.2, 0.15). Set the material to `InteractiveGrey`.

4. Lastly, give our critter some ears using two cylinders named `EarLeft` and `EarRight`, as children of `Mole`. Set their **Transform** to **Rotation** (−90, 0, 0) and **Scale** (0.05, 0.005, 0.05). For the position, try (−0.06, 0.35, 0.025) and (0.06, 0.35, 0.025). Set the materials to `InteractiveGrey`.

We limit our gray box object to the bare necessities. In this case, these objects are enough to illustrate a rough size and shape for our object. The addition of the ears, and reduced z-scaling will help detect any errant rotation of the otherwise symmetrical shape.

5. Add a Capsule Collider component to the `Mole` GameObject. Adjust the settings to match the following values, Capsule Collider settings:
   - Center = (0, 0.17, 0)
   - Radius = 0.09
   - Height = 0.43
   - Direction = Y-Axis

If you are using a different `mole` object, the Capsule Collider should be sized slightly larger than the asset. It represents the zone where a *hit* will be registered when our mallet collider intersects with the mole collider:

6. Save the scene.
7. Add a Rigidbody component to the `MolePosition (1)` and set the value to:
    - **Use Gravity** = Off
    - **Is Kinematic** = Off
    - **Interpolate** = None
    - **Collision Detection** = Continuous Dynamic
    - **Freeze Position** = all values checked **On**
    - **Freeze Rotation** = all values checked **On**

8. Add a new script to `MolePosition (1)` called `MoleController`. Move the `MoleController` script to the `Scripts` folder.

This script will control the mole's behavior. It will be used to determine when each mole pops up and what happens when the mallet collides with the mole's capsule collider. We will come back to define this script after building the scoring mechanism, mole animator, and animation state machine.

The Score Board

The challenge of our game will be to see how many moles the player can hit within 30 seconds. This will be challenging because the moles will pop up at random intervals across a wide area. Our intention is to create an enjoyable experience, but we will not be able to evaluate *fun* until we have a playable game.

The Score Board will be our tool for presenting the time remaining and the number of moles dispatched. It is created with a series of UI text elements that will be updated by a game controller script:

1. Add a **UI | Canvas** to the `MoleGame` GameObject and change its name to `ScoreBoard`.
2. First set the **Render Mode** to **World Space**. Setting the **Render Mode** first is required to provide access to the object's Rect Transform.
3. Set the Rect Transform to the following values:
    - Position = (0, `0.6`, `0.55`)
    - Width = `100`

- Height = 100
- Scale = (0.01, 0.01, 1)

These values should position the board slightly behind the table with its bottom edge just below the table top surface. Refer to *Figure 8.1* as a guide.

4. Add a **UI | Image** to the ScoreBoard GameObject. Rename the object ScoreBackground. This will create a white background to the ScoreBoard. Feel free to change the color setting or deactivate the Image component to match the aesthetic of your environment.

5. Add another child to the ScoreBoard. This should be a **UI | Text** element titled Timer. Set the attributes as:
    - **Width** = 90
    - **Alignment** = Center Top
    - **Horizontal Overflow** = Overflow
    - **Vertical Overflow** = Overflow

6. Make two duplicates of the Timer element, named Labels and Score.

7. Change the default values for the Text components to match the following:
    - **Timer** = 00:30
    - **Score** = 0
    - **Label** = Timer <return>Score

8. Arrange the elements as you see fit. Apply line spacing attributes to spread out the Label text. Again, *Figure 8.1* might be a helpful guide when laying out the score board typography.

Crispy UI Text

In Chapter 7, *Carnival Midway – Games Part 1*, we presented a process for producing sharp 3D type. UI Text requires a different approach. The following steps are optional and require importing new font assets:

1. Visit 1001freefonts.com or Fontspring.com to locate and download font faces for the label, score, and timer text fields. Select TrueType (.ttf files) or OpenType (.otf files) fonts for the best results.

2. Import the font files into Unity and move the assets to our `Font` folder.

3. Select each font and increase the **Font Size** from `16` to `90` in the **Inspector** panel.

4. Select `MoleGame | ScoreBoard | Timer`. Change the Rect Transform scale to (`0.25, 0.25, 0.25`). Increase the Text (Script) **Font Size** to `150`.

5. Repeat this process for the `Labels` and `Score` elements.

The mallet

The next prop is the mallet, but let's clarify what we mean by a mallet. Mallets are typically long hammer-style tools used in woodworking or croquet. In carnival games, a mallet is used to hit or smash things for points and prizes. But in our virtual world, a mallet can take any shape you desire. For our purposes, the more outlandish the shape the better the experience. *Figure 8.3* shows a few different mallet ideas, but we highly recommend being creative and experimenting with different shapes:

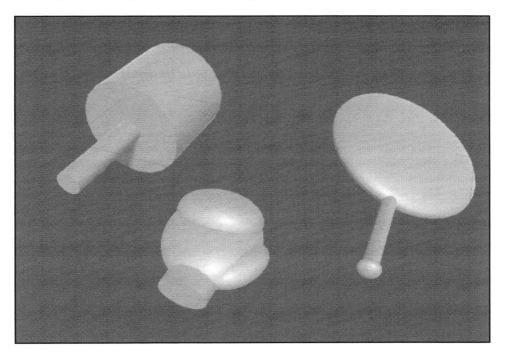

Figure 8.3: Various mallet shapes: mallet, boxing glove, and paddle

Whichever shape you use, there are a few components needed to interact correctly with scene elements. First there are the colliders. These are needed to determine if two objects touch each other. Later we will edit the MoleController script to recognize a collision and update the Score Board accordingly. But for that script to work, we need to make sure our mallet has at least one (mesh, box, or capsule) collider attached to the outermost GameObject container.

And secondly, we need the OVRGrabbable script. OVRGrabbable provides the ability to grab and throw objects. This script is amazing in that it handles so many situations and is as easy to use as any *drag and drop* tool. We only need to adjust a few attributes when applying the script to our mallet. For more information on the OVRGrabble script, visit the Oculus Utilities for Unity web page at https://developer.oculus.com/documentation/unity/latest/concepts/unity-utilities-overview/.

The following steps illustrate how to build and set up the typical carnival mallet. But the sky is the limit, and we hope you will explore other options as well:

1. Add a new empty GameObject to the MoleGame asset. Rename the object Mallet and position it near the GameTable.
2. Add the Rigidbody component to the new GameObject.
3. Add a new Cylinder to the Mallet GameObject, rename the object MalletHead, and set its rotation and scale as indicated here:
   - **Rotation** = (0, 0, 90)
   - **Scale** = (0.2, 0.09, 0.2)

4. Duplicate the MalletHead. Change its name to MalletHandle and set its scale to (0.05, 0.21, 0.05).
5. Reposition the MalletHandle to create the desired shape.
6. Select the Mallet GameObject and add the OVRGrabbable script from the OVR/Scripts/Util directory.

With the basic props in place, we can reactivate the Midway environment. Select the Environment, WackyMoles, and TeleportSystem GameObjects and reactivate them in the **Hierarchy** panel:

1. Transform the MoleGame to fit in the WackyMole booth. For our scene, we used the following values:
   - **Position** = (0, 1.05, −1.35)
   - **Rotation** = (−15, 0, 0)
   - **Scale** = (0.75, 0.75, 0.75)

2. Select the `MoleGame | ScoreBoard` and set its Rotation to (15, 0, 0). In the previous step, the Score Board was rotated forward to give the player better access to the game area. This step rotates the Score Board back to a vertical position.

3. Relocate the `MoleGame | Mallet` object so that it is sitting over the counter of the `WackyMole` booth. When the game is running, the mallet will drop down to the counter.

4. Drag the `MoleGame` GameObject into the `WackyMoles` object to keep everything organized.

Animating the mole

Our moles will randomly popup from their holes so that the player can bash them with the mallet. To do this, we have to build a simple animator which tells the mole how and when to move:

1. Create a new folder called `Animators` in the **Project** panel.

2. Select **Window | Animation** from the main menu. We will use this window to set keyframes for the `Mole` GameObject's position.

The **Animation** window (shown in *Figure 8. 4*) is used to create animation clips for individual GameObjects. The following steps involve creating the *popup* animation for our mole. For the *pop-down* animation, we will play this animation in reverse:

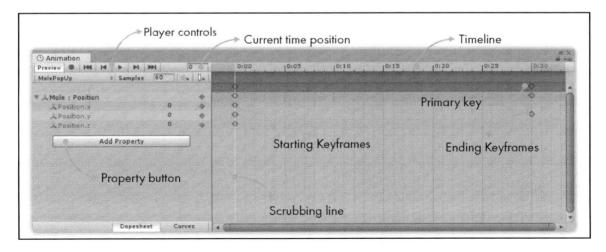

Figure 8.4: Components of the timeline window

3. With the **Animation** window open, select the `MoleGame | MolePosition (1) | Mole` GameObject. When a GameObject is selected, the **Animation** window will show a **Create** button.

4. Click the **Create** button and set the **Animation** name to `MolePopUp.anim` in the Create New Animation dialog. Put the animation clip in the `Animators` folder.

5. Click the Add Property button to reveal the properties to be animated.

6. Drill down to **Transform | Position** and click the plus sign (+) for Position. This will add the Position property and entries for `Position.x`, `Position.y`, and `Position.z` values. *Figure 8. 4* shows each of these values are set to `0`.

One animation technique utilized by the Unity engine is a keyframe animation. This method is used to smoothly transition scene objects over time. To animate an object, we create at least two keyframes on a timeline: a starting keyframe and an ending keyframe. These keyframes set transformation properties that tell the game engine *at this point in time put this object at (x^1, y^1, z^1).* Then at another point on the timeline, we set more keyframes that tell the engine *now at this time, transform the object to (x^2, y^2, z^2).* In this fashion, we can animate position, rotation, and scale for GameObjects, colliders, and mesh renders. The method is called keyframing because we only set *key* frames and the software generates the in-between frames, creating smooth transitions:

1. Scale the **Animation** window so that you can see both the starting and ending keyframes. In Unity 2017.3, the default keyframes are added at `0` and `1:00`.

2. Drag the primary key, located in the dark gray area above the timeline grid, from `1:00` to `0:30`. This will move the ending keyframes (`Position.x`, `Position.y`, and `Position.z`) to the new position, changing the animation duration from one full-second to half-second.

3. Click the timeline at `0:00` to reposition the scrub line. Changing keyframes requires the scrub line to be parked at the time where the change needs to occur.

4. Click the `0` in the Position.y property field and change the value to `-0.4`.

5. Hit the Play button in the **Animation** window to view the clip.

Our brief animation plays. Adjust the keyframe values if your mole doesn't recede completely below the `GameTable`'s surface.

6. Stop the animation by clicking Play button again.

7. Select the `MolePopUp` clip in the **Project** window and uncheck the **Loop Time** checkbox. Because we will use a script to control the mole, we will not need to loop the animation.

Our animation is done. But Unity doesn't know how to handle the clip. If you hit the Scene Play button, you'll see the mole move, but it only pops up. It never recedes back into position; the animation clip cuts short and replays from the beginning. We are going to fix this with the state machine.

A state machine provides additional control for our animations. In the Zombie Shooting Gallery project, we used a state machine to control when each animation is triggered. Here we will use the function to control the pop-up and pop-down states.

Building an animation state machine

Let's look at the `Animators` folder in the **Project** window. You will notice that although we created the animation clips, the folder also has a state machine. This will give us a leg up for the next step of the process:

1. Double-click the mole state machine. The default state machine window, as shown in *Figure 8. 5*, will already have the `MolePopUp` animation clip attached to the Entry node:

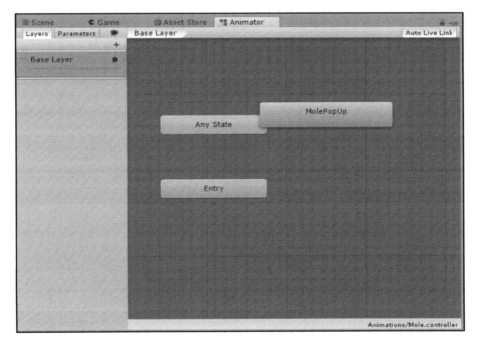

Figure 8.5: Starting the state machine window

2. Right-click in the grid space and select Create **State** | **Empty**.

3. Rename the `New State` item Default in the **Inspector** panel.

4. Create another new state called `MolePopDown`.

5. Right-click the Default state and select **Set as Layer Default State**. This will change the start to Orange and the transition arrow will switch from `MolePopUp` to Default.

6. Right-click the Default state again and choose **Make transitions**. Immediately click on the `MolePopUp` state to identify the transition point. A new arrow will appear between Default and `MolePopUp`.

7. Repeat this process to create a transition from `MolePopUp` to `MolePopDown` and another from `MolePopDown` to `MolePopUp`.

8. Click the **Parameters** tab in the upper-left side of the window.

9. Create a Boolean variable by clicking the small (+) drop-down button in the upper-left corner of the **Parameters** tab and set its name to `isActive`.

10. Create a second Boolean parameter called `wasActive`.

Select the `MolePopUp` state. The **Inspector** window should show that the Motion field value is `MolePopUp`. This was the clip we created in the *Build an animator* section. The following steps are optional and should only be followed if the Motion field is not set to `MolePopUp`:

1. Click the selection target for the `Motion` field. A window will open with a list of animation clips.

2. Since our project only has one clip, double-click `MolePopUp` to set the value.

3. Select the `MolePopDown` state and set the `MolePopUp` motion field to the `MolePopUp` clip.

4. Change the **Speed** attribute from 1 to -1. Setting the speed to a negative value will cause the clip to play at 100% speed in reverse.

The last steps for the state machine will tell our mole when to transition from popping up to popping down. We will do this in the **Inspector** panel for the transition arrows:

1. Select the Default to `MolePopUp` arrow.

2. Locate the *Conditions* section in the **Inspector** panel. Note that the list is empty.

3. Click the (+) sign to add a condition to the transition.

Conditions are used by the state machine to determine when a transition should occur. Transitions can be assigned one, none, or multiple conditions. When assigned, all conditions in the list must be satisfied before the transition is triggered:

1. Add the following conditions and values to the selected transition arrow:
   - Uncheck the **Has Exit Time** checkbox
   - **isActive** = true
   - **wasActive** = false

2. Select the `MolePopDown` to `MolePopUp` transition arrow and set the following values:
   - Uncheck the **Has Exit Time** checkbox
   - `isActive` = **true**
   - `wasActive` = **false**

3. Set the following conditions for the `MolePopUp` to `MolePopDown` transition arrow:
   - Uncheck the **Has Exit Time** checkbox
   - **isActive** = false
   - **wasActive** = true

Figure 8. 6 shows the completed state machine. Verify the transitional arrows conditions, and the **Motion** and **Speed** for each state:

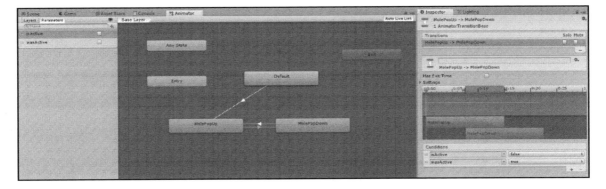

Figure 8.6: Final state machine showing parameters and transition conditions

If you hit Scene Play now, our mole would not pop up. This is as expected, because our state machine is waiting for the `isActive` Boolean to get a TRUE value. We will add this functionality in the `MoleController` script.

4. Save the scene.

Scripting the mole asset

The next phase of this project is to construct the controller script for the mole. We will tackle the script in chunks, with descriptions to provide more information on the purpose of each method and function:

1. Double-click the `MoleController` script.

2. Modify the script to add the necessary variables:

```
using System.Collections;
 using System.Collections.Generic;
 using UnityEngine;

public class MoleController : MonoBehaviour {
    [SerializeField] float popupSpeed;
    [SerializeField] float distanceToRaise;
    float maxMoleTime = 4f;

    Animator animator;
    AudioSource audioSource;

    bool canActivate = true;
    bool isActivated = false;
    bool wasActivated = false;

    IEnumerator runningCoroutine;

    int timesHasBeenWhacked = 0;
```

3. The `Start()` function sets the values of the animator and `audioSource` to their initial values:

```
void Start() {
    animator = GetComponentInChildren<Animator>();
    audioSource = GetComponent<AudioSource>();
}
```

4. The `Update()` function checks for the current condition of the mole on each frame. With this information, we can time when the audio should play:

```
void Update() {
    animator.SetBool("isActive", isActivated);
    animator.SetBool("wasActive", wasActivated);

    if ((wasActivated && !isActivated) || (!wasActivated &&
    isActivated)) {
        float assumedSampleRate = 44100f;
        float animationLength =
        animator.GetCurrentAnimatorStateInfo(0).length;

    }

    wasActivated = isActivated;
}
```

5. The next three functions, `ResetGame`, `StartGame`, and `StopGame`, evoke co-routines that trigger the fourth function, `RandomlyToggle`. This function randomly sets the animation start time for each mole. In practice, this means that each mole pops up at different times, creating a challenging experience for our players:

```
public void ResetGame() {
    StopCoroutine(RandomlyToggle());
}

public void StartGame() {
    StartCoroutine(RandomlyToggle());
}

public void StopGame() {
    StopCoroutine(RandomlyToggle());
}

IEnumerator RandomlyToggle() {
    float randomTimeLength = Random.Range(0f, maxMoleTime);
    yield return new WaitForSeconds(randomTimeLength);
    if (canActivate) {
    isActivated = !isActivated;
}
    StartCoroutine(RandomlyToggle());
}
```

6. `DeactiveCooldown()` is used to add a pause to the mole's animation cycle. Without this, the moles would immediately pop up when they get hit:

```
IEnumerator DeactivateCooldown() {
    yield return new WaitForSeconds(1f);
    canActivate = true;
}
```

7. The last two functions control the mole's collision states. When the mole collides with an object with the `Player` tag, we change its conditions, increment the hit, and create a pause in the animation:

```
void OnCollisionEnter(Collision other) {
    if (isActivated && other.GameObject.tag == "Player") {
        isActivated = false;
        canActivate = false;
        timesHasBeenWhacked++;
        StartCoroutine(DeactivateCooldown());
    }
}

public int TimesBeenWhacked {
    get {
        return timesHasBeenWhacked;
    }
}
}
```

8. Save and close the script.
9. Return to Unity, and save the scene and project.

Scripting the mole game controller

Now we will focus on building a controller script for the mole game. This script will manage the Score Board text elements and the starting times for the moles:

1. Begin the process by creating a new script on the `MoleGame` GameObject. Name the script `MoleGameController`.
2. Double-click the new script to open it in your editor.

3. Modify the script to match the following functions and methods:

```
using System.Collections;
using System.Collections.Generic;
using UnityEngine;
using UnityEngine.UI;

public class MoleGameController : MonoBehaviour {

    [SerializeField] Text timerUI, scoreUI;
    [SerializeField] float startingTimeInSeconds = 30f;

    List<MoleController> moles;
    int score = 0;
    float timer = 0f;
    bool isTiming;

    void Start() {
        moles = new List<MoleController>();
        StartGame();
    }

    void Update() {
        int scoreAccumulator = 0;
        foreach (MoleController mole in
        GetComponentsInChildren<MoleController>()) {
        }

        score = scoreAccumulator;
        scoreUI.text = score.ToString();

        int minutesLeft = (int) Mathf.Clamp((startingTimeInSeconds -
        timer) / 60, 0, 99);
        int secondsLeft = (int) Mathf.Clamp((startingTimeInSeconds -
        timer) % 60, 0, 99);
        timerUI.text = string.Format("{0:D2}:{1:D2}", minutesLeft,
        secondsLeft);
    }

    void FixedUpdate() {
        if (isTiming) {
            timer += Time.deltaTime;
        }
    }

    public void StartGame() {
        foreach (MoleController mole in
```

```
        GetComponentsInChildren<MoleController>()) {
            moles.Add(mole);
            mole.StartGame();
        }
        StartTimer();
    }

    public void StopGame() {
        StopTimer();
    }

    // Starts Timer
    public void StartTimer() {
        timer = 0f;
        isTiming = true;
    }

    public void StopTimer() {
        isTiming = false;
    }
}
```

Selecting the `MoleGameObject` will reveal three public fields: `Timer UI`, `Score UI`, and `Starting Time`. `Starting Time` already has a default value, but the other two will need to be set before running the game.

4. Click the selection target for `Timer UI` and `Score UI` and set their values to the appropriate UI Text object.

Finishing the Wacky Mole game

With the animation and script complete, we can put the final touches on the Wacky Mole game:

1. Duplicate the `MolePosition (1)` asset to create critters appropriate for your game area.

For our example, we made a total of nine moles. The following table identifies a simple 3x3 grid for nine moles. Obviously, there are countless layouts that could be used; we are just providing this arrangement because it defines the layout we used in *Figure 8. 1*. The Y position for each of the `MolePosition` assets is 0, but the remaining objects can be positioned using this chart:

	Pos X = -0.3	Pos X = 0	Pos X = 0.3
Pos Z = 0.3	MolePosition (1)	MolePosition (2)	MolePosition (3)
Pos Z = 0	MolePosition (4)	MolePosition (5)	MolePosition (6)
Pos Z = -0.3	MolePosition (7)	MolePosition (8)	MolePosition (9)

2. Save the scene.
3. Run the game to test the results.
4. Hide the `WackyMoles` GameObject and unhide `BottleSmash`.

Milk Bottle Toss props

Typical Milk Bottle Toss games give the player two or three throws to knock down a small pyramid of milk bottles. These games require a great deal of accuracy and strength to win. Because like most Midway activities, the game is designed to greatly reduce your chance of winning. In this game, the bottom bottles often have lead plugs or are partially filled with sand making them too heavy to be easily toppled by the game's under-weighted (and sometimes corked-filled) softball. Of course, our game will be fair. The player will have five chances to knock down two milk bottle pyramids.

For this game, we won't be learning anything new. Instead we will be using the `OVRGrabbable` script from the `WackyMoles` game to facilitate throwing softballs. This interaction will be very simple, but rewarding to the player. Consider this when designing your own VR experiences.

Game props

Our version of the traditional game will be simpler, but it still requires a good bit of dexterity to win. The five-bottle pyramids will be placed when the game is launched and restacked when needed. We will provide the player with five balls that can be picked up and thrown with the Touch controller. And lastly, we'll add a reset button to remove the thrown balls and lay out a new set for the player to throw:

1. Create an empty GameObject called BottleGame at (0, 0, 0).

2. Just like we did with the MoleGame, we need to assign a new script to the BottleGame called BottleGameController. This script will instantiate the balls and bottles, and facilitate a reset function.

   Our Milk Bottle Toss game (the BottleSmash GameObject) booth is no longer at the origin. But we will build the needed props and then relocate the BottleGameObject to the proper position. The first items we need will support the game props. The Runner items will provide a rail system to keep the balls from rolling away from the player. And the BottlePlatform is a thin cube where the bottle pyramids will rest.

3. Add three cubes, RunnerFront, RunnerBack, and BottlePlatform as children to the BottleGame. The Runners will be used to keep the balls in position on the platform and the BottlePlatform will hold our bottle pyramid prefabs. Transform the cubes to match the following settings:

	Position	Rotation	Scale
RunnerFront	0, 0.9, -1.9	0, 0, 0	3.4, 0.06, 0.02
RunnerBack	0, 0.9, -1.8	0, 0, 0	3.4, 0.06, 0.02
BottlePlatform	0, 0.9, 0.23	0, 0, 0	4, 0.03, 0.4

4. Reposition the BottleGame GameObject to sit within the BottleSmash. Use *Figure 8.7* as a guide. The actual location will depend on the Midway booth layout designed in Chapter 7, *Carnival Midway – Games Part 1*.

5. The next props are the ball and bottle. Use the following simple shapes to craft the placeholders as children of the `BottleGame`. The ball should be placed between the `Runner` objects and the bottle should sit on the platform near the middle:

	Shape	Scale
`Ball`	Sphere	`0.07,0.07,0.07`
`Bottle`	Cylinder	`0.1,0.13,0.1`

6. Add a RigidBody component to the `Ball` and `Bottle` GameObjects. Make sure **Use Gravity** is checked and **Collision Detection** is set to **Continuous Dynamic** for both objects.

By default, cylinders have a Capsule collider. This collider can be adjusted for multiple uses, but it will still have a rounded base and crown. These attributes prevent the object from standing on its end and would make it impossible to construct a pyramid. Instead we will replace it with a Mesh collider. We often use the Mesh collider for complex shapes, but in this instance, we are relying on its ability to use the object's Mesh Rendered to create a collider:

1. Remove the Bottle's Capsule collider and replace it by adding a Mesh collider. Set the **Convex** attribute to on by checking the box.
2. Add the OVR Grabbable script to the `Ball` GameObject. As we saw when creating the mallet, this script facilitates grabbing and throwing of GameObjects.
3. Hit Play to test the scene.

 It is important to use the Touch controller's safety straps. Throwing an object requires a bit of dexterity gymnastics. The Grip buttons allow us to hold objects, but timing the release of the button with a forward-throwing motion requires practice.

At this point, we can pick up and throw the ball. And with some practice, you can improve your aim and timing. In the game, we will need to hit a pyramid of bottles and clear them from the platform. The following props are made by duplicating the `Ball` and `Bottle` we have already created.

4. Create two new empty GameObjects, `FiveBalls` and a `BottlePyramid`, to hold our props.

A secondary goal of our game is to create an environment that can be reset during runtime. There are several methods to achieve this, but the solution we have defined here is straightforward and the most approachable for a wide variety of developer skill sets.

The `Five Balls` and `BottlePyramid` GameObjects will contain several primitive shapes arranged in the scene. Once the objects are complete, they will be converted to prefabs. As prefabs, we will be able to store their initial starting positions, interact with them during gameplay, and reset the scene, giving players multiple chances to improve their skill and win the game:

1. Move the `Ball` GameObject into `FiveBalls`. Duplicate it four times and place them between the runners as shown in *Figure 8. 9*.

2. Move the `Bottle` GameObject into the `BottlePyramid`. Duplicate and arrange the objects into pyramids. *Figure 8. 7* shows that we created three pyramids of six bottles, but feel free to adjust this to meet your own design:

Figure 8.7: Layout of completed **Milk Bottle Toss** props

3. Create two new tags: balls and bottles. Assign the balls tag to `FiveBalls` and the bottles tag to `BottlePyramids`.

4. Drag `FiveBalls` into the `Project/Prefabs` folder to create a prefab.

5. Repeat the process for the `BottlePyramids`.

6. Save the scene.

Scripting the Milk Bottle Toss game

The script for this game is very simple and basic in nature. Without a scoring mechanism or need for a state machine, the script is just a shell to house the reset function.

While the game is running, the script *listens* for the Touch Controller's *B* or *Y* buttons. If either of these are pushed, the script destroys the balls and bottles from the scene and replaces them with new prefabs. It is a very fast solution which is easy to follow:

1. Open the `BottleGameController` script and edit it to match the following. The script starts by setting variables for the prefabs and the transforms:

```
using System.Collections;
using System.Collections.Generic;
using UnityEngine;

 public class BottleGameController : MonoBehaviour {
     [SerializeField] GameObject BottlePyramidPrefab;
     [SerializeField] GameObject FiveBallsPrefab;

     private Vector3 PryamidPosition;
     private Quaternion PryamidRotation;
     private Vector3 BallsPosition;
     private Quaternion BallsRotation;
```

In the `Start()` functions, we store the starting transforms for the bottle and ball prefabs. Storing these values will make it easier to position the new GameObjects after a reset:

```
    // Use this for initialization
    void Start () {
        PryamidPosition =
        GameObject.FindWithTag("bottles").transform.position;
        PryamidRotation =
        GameObject.FindWithTag("bottles").transform.rotation;
        BallsPosition =
        GameObject.FindWithTag("balls").transform.position;
        BallsRotation =
```

```
        GameObject.FindWithTag("balls").transform.rotation;
    }
```

The Update() function, which is called during every frame in runtime, listens for the *B* and *Y* buttons to be pushed. When this happens, we destroy the current GameObjects and instantiate new versions, using the starting transforms of the original prefabs. Once the new objects are created, we set their tags so that they can be removed during the next reset activity:

```
// Update is called once per frame
void Update () {
    if (Input.GetButtonDown("Button.Two") ||
        Input.GetButtonDown("Button.Four")) {
        Destroy (GameObject.FindWithTag("bottles"));
        Destroy (GameObject.FindWithTag("balls"));

        GameObject BottlePryamids = Instantiate
        (BottlePyramidPrefab, PryamidPosition, PryamidRotation);
        GameObject FiveBalls = Instantiate (FiveBallsPrefab,
        BallsPosition, BallsRotation);

        BottlePryamids.tag = "bottles";
        FiveBalls.tag = "balls";
    }
  }
}
```

1. Save the script and return to Unity.
2. Select the `BottleGame` GameObject which houses the game's props. Notice the prefab fields in the **Inspector** panel.
3. Drag the `BottlePyramids` and `FiveBalls` prefabs from the `Prefab` folder to the appropriate fields of the Bottle Game Controller component, as shown in *Figure 8.8*:

 Important: Drag each prefab from the folder and not the GameObjects in the **Hierarchy** window. Using the scene GameObjects will cause an error at runtime.

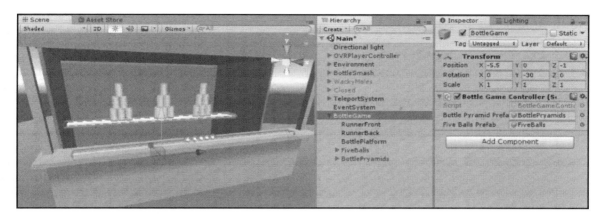

Figure 8.8: Assigning the prefabs for the BottleGameController script

4. Save the scene and project.
5. Hit Play to test the scene.
6. If all runs smoothly, activate all hidden objects.

Building the application

I am still amazed at how easy it is to build an executable application in Unity. This is a testament to the constant improvements made by the development staff. These improvements aid in all aspects of development, including building the application:

1. Choose **Build Settings** from the **File** menu.
2. Confirm that the target platform is set to Windows and the current scene is listed in the **Scenes In Build** panel.
3. Click the **Build** button and save the .exe file to a new location. It is common practice to create a Builds directory at the top level of the project folder, alongside (but not inside) the Asset directory.

4. Launch the application and marvel at your work:

Figure 8.9: Carnival booths

Expanding the game

The steps provided here serve to build a prototypical midway experience for virtual reality. But you don't have to stop here. Consider making the following improvements:

- Add sounds: Incorporate ambient crowd noises, carnival music at the booths, the sound of the mallet hitting a mole, or the ball hitting a bottle.
- Add a scoring UI: Remove the UI Canvas from the mole game and add a scoring mechanism to the VR camera.
- Design a new game for the closed booth: How about a dart/archery activity, basketball hoops, Skee-Ball, Ring Toss, or WaterGun game? Or something entirely new that is only possible in VR.
- Move on to the next phase: Replace our primitive GameObjects with 3D modeled shapes and textures. Build new objects in a 3D application or search the Asset Store for suitable GameObjects.

Summary

Our goal in this project was to introduce the novice reader to many commonly used VR techniques and best practices. Our investigation began preproduction planning and design. In this phase, we looked at planning the experience and setting up the Unity environment for VR development, which included a look at the Oculus Virtual Reality plugin. This package contains scripts and prefabs for facilitating VR interactions, camera management, grasping with Touch Controllers, haptic response, debugging tools, and an avatar system.

With the OVR elements in place, we looked at the level design technique of *gray boxing*. This is an early design technique used to prototype our scene, focusing on mechanics, movement, and interaction. Instead of finished models, textures, and visual effects, we reduced our palette to primitive shapes, grayscale colors, and simple materials. Without the distraction of the environment's aesthetics, this process lets us focus on the environment's entertainment value over its *look and feel*.

From here we set about building the play areas, props, animations' and scripts to facilitate user interactions. Along the way, we donned the Rift headset to conduct functional testing, adjusting and tweaking our scene as needed. Many of the choices were left to the reader to add their own creative spin to the project.

As a prelude to constructing a player movement system, we discussed procedures for combating VR sickness/discomfort. Building on 30+ years of work done by researchers and industry developers, we presented six key procedures for creating comfortable experiences. These simple principles provide the reader with valuable guidelines for future VR projects and the tools needed to build a teleport system within the Midway project.

From there the project moved on to building the game props and scripts to play the games. The skills and techniques addressed in this project go well beyond the uses we illustrated in this project. VR is being used to train employees, explore data in new ways, and help businesses improve their support and services. With practice and creativity, we expect you to go out and find uses for VR in your professional and social life.

Instead of whacking moles, consider creating a physical therapy game that measures a player's recover rate after surgery. Or, with a few adjustments, the same script can be used to train factory workers on new equipment and procedures. Or maybe you want to build a virtual interface for a physical system. We urge you to think beyond the technology and instead consider the broader possibilities presented in virtual reality.

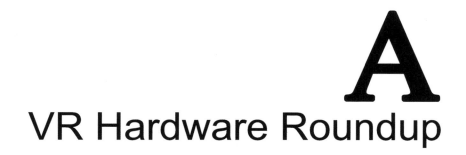 VR Hardware Roundup

Since its early inception, virtual reality has offered an escape. Donning a headset can transport you to a brand new world, full of wonderment and excitement. Or it can let you explore a location too dangerous for human existence. Or it can even just present the real world to you in a new manner. And now that we have moved past the era of bulky goggles and clumsy helmets, the hardware is making the aim of unfettered escapism a reality.

VR hardware roundup

In this Appendix, we wanted to present a *roundup* of the modern VR hardware systems. Each product is presented giving an overview of the device, an image, and its price as of February 2018. Please use this information to compare systems and find the device which best suits your personal needs.

There has been an explosion of VR hardware in the last three years. They range from cheaply made housings around a pair of lens to full headsets with embedded screens creating a 110-degree field of view. Each device offers distinct advantages and use cases. Many have even dropped significantly in price over the past 12 months making them more accessible to a wider audience of users. Following is a brief overview of each device, ranked in terms of price and complexity.

Google Cardboard

Cardboard VR is compatible with a wide range of contemporary smartphones.

Google Cardboard's biggest advantage is its low cost, broad hardware support, and portability. As a bonus, it is wireless.

Using the phone's gyroscopes, the VR applications can track the user in 360 degrees of rotation.

While modern phones are very powerful, they are not as powerful as desktop PCs. But the user is untethered and the systems are lightweight:

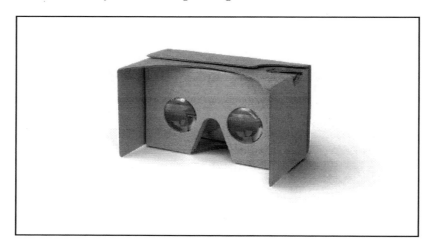

http://www.vr.google.com/cardboard/

Cost: $5-20 (plus an iOS or Android smartphone)

Google Daydream

Rather than plastic, the Daydream is built from a fabric-like material and is bundled with a Wii-like motion controller with a trackpad and buttons.

It does have superior optics compared to a Cardboard, but is not as nice as the higher end VR systems.

Just as with the Gear VR, it works only with a very specific list of phones:

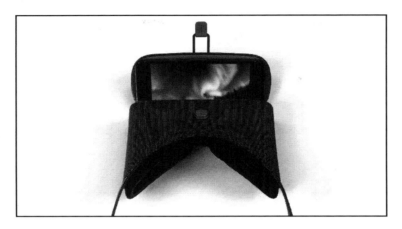

`http://www.vr.google.com/daydream/`

Cost: $79 (plus a Google or Android Smartphone)

Gear VR

Gear VR is part of the Oculus ecosystem. While it still uses a smartphone (Samsung only), the Gear VR HMD includes some of the same circuitry from the Oculus Rift PC solution. This results in far more responsive and superior tracking compared to Google Cardboard, although it still only tracks rotation:

http://www3.oculus.com/en-us/gear-vr/

Cost: $99 (plus Samsung Android Smartphone)

Oculus Rift

The Oculus Rift is the platform that reignited the VR renaissance through its successful Kickstarter campaign. The Rift uses a PC and external cameras that allow not only rotational tracking, but also positional tracking, allowing the user a full VR experience. The Samsung relationship allows Oculus to use Samsung screens in their HMDs.

While the Oculus no longer demands that the user remain seated, it does want the user to move within a smaller 3 m x 3 m area. The Rift HMD is wired to the PC.

The user can interact with the VR world with the included Xbox gamepad, mouse and keyboard, a one-button clicker, or proprietary wireless controllers:

http://www3.oculus.com/en-us/rift/

Cost: $399 plus $800 for a VR-ready PC

Vive

The HTC Vive from Valve uses smartphone panels from HTC.

The Vive has its own proprietary wireless controllers, of a different design than Oculus (but it can also work with gamepads, joysticks, mouse/keyboards).

The most distinguishing characteristic is that the Vive encourages users to explore and walk within a 4 m x 4 m, or larger, cube:

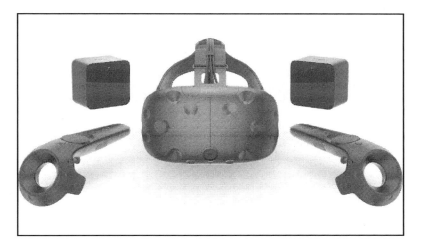

http://store.steampowered.com/vive/

Cost: $599 plus an $800 VR-ready PC

Sony PSVR

While there are persistent rumors of an Xbox VR HMD, Sony is currently the only video game console with a VR HMD.

It is easier to install and set up than a PC-based VR system, and while the library of titles is much smaller, the quality of the titles is higher overall on average. It is also the most affordable of the positional tracking VR options. But, it is also the only one that cannot be developed on by the average hobbyist developer:

https://www.gamestop.com/collection/playstation-vr

Cost: $400, plus Sony Playstation 4 console

HoloLens

Microsoft's HoloLens provides a unique AR experience in several ways.

The user is not blocked off from the *real world*; they can still see the world around them (other people, desks, chairs, and so on) through the HMD's semitransparent optics.

The HoloLens scans the user's environment and creates a 3D representation of that space. This allows the *Holograms* from the HoloLens to interact with objects in the room. Holographic characters can sit on couches in the room, fish can avoid table legs, screens can be placed on walls in the room, and so on.

The system is completely wireless. It's the only commercially available positional tracking device that is wireless. The computer is built into HMD with the processing power that sits in between a smartphone and a VR-ready PC.

The user can walk, untethered, in areas as large as 30 m x 30 m.

While an Xbox controller and a proprietary single-button controller can be used, the main interaction with the HoloLens is through voice commands and two gestures from the user's hand (Select and Go back).

The final difference is that the holograms only appear in a relatively narrow field of view.

Because the user can still see other people, either sharing the same Holographic projections or not, the users can interact with each other in a more natural manner:

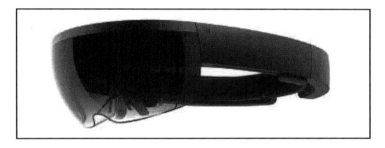

www.microsoft.com/microsoft-hololens/en-us

Cost: Development Edition: $3000; Commercial Suite: $5000

Headset costs

The following chart is a sampling of VR headset prices, accurate at of February 1, 2018. VR/AR hardware is rapidly advancing and prices and specs are going to change annually, sometimes quarterly. Just as this chapter was being written, the price of the Oculus dropped by $200:

	Google Cardboard	Gear VR	Google Daydream	Oculus Rift	HTC Vive	Sony PS VR	HoloLens
Complete cost for HMD, trackers, default controllers	$5	$99	$79	$399	$599	$299	$3000
Total cost with CPU: phone, PC, PS4	$200	$650	$650	$1,400	$1,500	$600	$3000
Built-in headphones	NO	No	No	Yes	No	No	Yes
Platform	Apple Android	Samsung Galaxy	Google Pixel	PC	PC	Sony PS4	Proprietary PC
Enhanced rotational tracking	No	Yes	No	Yes	Yes	Yes	yes
Positional tracking	No	No	No	Yes	Yes	Yes	Yes
Built-in touch panel	No*	Yes	No	No	No	No	no
Motion controls	No	No	No	Yes	Yes	Yes	Yes
Tracking system	No	No	No	Optical	Lighthouse	Optical	Laser

True 360 tracking	No	No	No	Yes	Yes	No	Yes
Room scale and size	No	No	No	Yes	Yes	Yes	Yes
Remote	No	No	Yes	Yes	No	No	Yes
Gamepad support	No	Yes	No	Yes 2m x 2m	Yes 4m x 4m	Yes 3m x 3m	Yes 10mX10m
Resolution per eye	Varies	1440 x1280	1440 x1280	1200 x1080	1200 x1080	1080 x960	1268 X720
Field of view	Varies	100	90	110	110	100	30
Refresh rate	60 Hz	60 Hz	60 Hz	90 Hz	90 Hz	90-120 Hz	60 Hz
Wireless	Yes	Yes	Yes	No	No	No	Yes
Optics adjustment	No	Focus	No	IPD	IPD	IPD	IPD
Operating system	iOS Android	Android Oculus	Android Daydream	Win 10 Oculus	Win 10 Steam	Sony PS4	Win 10
Built-in Camera	Yes	Yes	Yes*	No	Yes*	No	Yes
AR/VR	VR*	VR*	VR	VR	VR*	VR	AR
Natural user Interface	No	No	No	No	No		Yes

Choosing which HMD to support comes down to a wide range of issues: cost, access to hardware, use cases, image fidelity/processing power, and more. The previous chart is provided to help the user understand the strengths and weaknesses of each platform.

There are many HMDs not included in this overview. Some are not commercially available at the time of this writing (Magic Leap, the Win 10 HMD licensed from Microsoft, the Starbreeze/IMAX HMD, and others) and some are not yet widely available or differentiated enough: Razer's Open Source HMD.

B
VR Terms and Definitions

Virtual reality and augmented reality have seen billions of dollars in investments in the last five years from some of the largest tech companies (Google, Facebook, Microsoft, Sony, and Samsung, for instance), giving the Sci-Fi stalwart a second lease of life.

VR terms and definitions

For the purposes of this book, we will define **augmented reality (AR)** as the melding of the real-world environment and **computer generated imagery (CGI)**. AR is more than just a simple **Heads Up Display (HUD)**, as AR tracks some or all of the real-world environment in three dimensions in real time, giving the impression that the computer generate imagery is part of the real world. Simple AR demos populate the App Stores for all modern smartphones, though the best experiences are done through a **Head Mounted Display (HMD)**.

In AR, a CGI cartoon character would be drawn in your living room. With certain AR hardware, all of the details in your living room would be scanned and converted into 3D spatial data, allowing the CGI cartoon character to interact with your furniture, jumping from the floor to the couch, to the coffee table. You would see both your living room and the cartoon character interacting together in three dimensions, and doing so accurately.

One of the advantages of AR is that it can require a far less powerful processing system, in large part because so much of the viewer's experience does not need to be drawn by the computer. AR is supposed to augment your reality, not replace it. So instead of having to calculate and draw all of a world, an AR game need only draw the characters that interact with it. There's no point in drawing the couch, if the AR character is going to jump on it.

Virtual Reality (VR) replaces your entire field of view with CGI. In your living room, in VR, you would no longer see your couch and coffee table. No mater where you looked, a new world would be drawn for you. You could see the interior of a medieval castle, or the triptychs of Stonehenge, or the plains of Mars.

In the 1990s, long-forgotten companies such as Virtual iO, CyberMaxx, and VPL tried to move VR from the pages of science fiction into the living rooms. While impressive technology for their time, their low resolution (320 x 200), flat shaded images rendered at less than 30 frames per second and high costs of $800 (not adjusted for inflation), were not enough to satisfy consumers and, other than at research institutions and in a few high end markets, the products vanished:

But in 2012, VR got a new lease of life via the intersection of high-resolution smartphone screens, home computer power, and crowdsourcing. Crowdsourcing meant that VR did not need approval from large corporations and the large sales numbers they need to bring a product to market. The money could be raised directly from consumers, allowing for small, niche products to be funded. This was perfect for VR, which for a long time had a small, but passionate fan base, willing to help fund the dream of VR.

The success of Oculus was quickly followed by Vive from Valve, HoloLens from Microsoft, and a host of others. An arms race to what many view will be the next big thing, possibly the biggest thing ever, has begun:

- **Engine support**: Unity has built-in support for all of the HMDs listed previously. Unreal has built-in support for every HMD, except the HoloLens.
- **Complete cost (for HMD, trackers, default controllers):** This is the complete cost of the base system required to do all that is promised. For example, the **PlayStation VR (PSVR)** can be purchased without the required cameras and wands, but few people have those items. So the true cost is the cost of the HMD, the camera, and the wands. The first publicly available Oculus system, the DK2, was a single-sensor, sit-down system that used a wired Xbox game controller (sold separately) for user input. The current version of the Rift, the CV1, is a two-sensor system with two wireless controllers, for $399.00.
- **Total cost with processor: phone, PC, PS4:** This represents the lowest total cost of the HMD and processing system to run for the minimum required specification. For example, one could spend far more than $800 for a minimum spec VR PC or more than $300 for a Sony PS4.
- **Built-in headphones**: All the HMDs support audio, but only two have built-in head phones: The Rift and the HoloLens. The audio design of the HoloLens isn't based on traditional headphones at all; they are more like little *sound projectors* that leave the ears uncovered, better allowing one to interact with the real world, while allowing audio from the computer world to also be heard. All of the smartphone-based options can support headphones/ear buds or can emit sound from the phone itself. There is an additional audio strap available for the Vive, which costs $99.
- **Platform**: What is the main hardware platform required to run the system?
- **Enhanced positional tracking**: Google Cardboard and Daydream use the gyroscopics of phones to track head tilt and rotation. The Gear is not just a plastic version of Google Cardboard. The Gear has additional hardware in the HMD to make its tracking more responsive and accurate than that of Google Cardboard. The Rift, Vive, and HoloLens use their tracking systems to improve the latency and accuracy even more.

- **Positional tracking**: All of the systems support rotational tracking (looking up/down and all around). None of the phone-based systems (Cardboard, Daydream, Gear) support positional tracking (moving the head up/down and across the room); at least, not yet. This is expected to change very rapidly over the coming 2 years; as smartphones become more powerful, the move will be from *outside in* tracking (where cameras outside the HMD track its location) to *inside out* tracking (where the HMD itself tracks its own location). Currently only the HoloLens does inside out tracking.

- **Built-in touch panel**: The Gear has a trackpad built into the right side of the HMD, allowing the user to make a simple gesture input, simple joypad input, and single and double tap input. The official Google Cardboard has a single button, but its low-cost production make the button unreliable.

- **Motion controls**: Does the system ship with and support 6 DOF (degree of freedom) motion controls in its complete cost price point? The Vive, Rift, and PSVR all support motion controls.

- **Tracking system**: How is the HMD (and controllers) tracked? The HoloLens uses a system not unlike the Kinect to scan the world and build a spatial map with its **Holographic Processing Unit (HPU)**. The Rift and PSVR use cameras to track the HMD and controllers. The Vive uses lasers to scan the environment from its Lighthouse system.

- **True 360 tracking**: Can the user turn completely around and still be tracked accurately? The Vive, Rift, and HoloLens do support full 360 degree tracking. The PSVR, comes close, but because it only has a single camera, it cannot track a full 360 degrees.

- **Room scale and size**: If the system can support room scale positional movement, what is the size (in meters), they can support? The HoloLens, the only wireless system currently available, can support a very large space. I have used it in basketball court size spaces. The Vive, Rift, and PSVR are restricted by the cable length's as well as the positions of the optical systems required to track the HMD.

- **Remote:** The HoloLens, Rift, and Daydream ship with a one-button, clicker style, remote. It can be used as an input device. Gear VR has announced a similar remote to ship later in 2017.

- **Gamepad support**: Will the system work with a traditional console, twin stick gamepad (similar to an Xbox or PS3 controller)? As both the Vive and Rift are PC-based, they have supported gamepad (and mouse and keyboard) inputs. The Rift shipped with an Xbox One controller for its first year. The Gear VR briefly had an official gamepad, and will still work with Bluetooth controllers. The HoloLens, being a Microsoft product, also supports the Xbox One controllers. The PSVR has some games that will work with PS4 gamepads.

- **Resolution per eye**: How many pixels are displayed to each eye? The more pixels, the better the image, but the more processing power that is required.

- **Field of view**: How much of our field of view does the HMD fill? The human eyes' have a field of view of over 180 degrees, although the fidelity of our peripheral vision is not as acute as it is at the center; so while HMD designers could increase the FOV beyond their current 100 degree range, they would do so by spreading more pixels across a larger area, making the image lower resolution/more pixilated. But many believe a wider FOV is key for a more immersive experience.

- **Refresh rate**: How fast are the images drawn on the display panel? 30 FPS (frames per second) is the minimum required to not see flicker, although the periphery of our eyesight can perceive flicker at higher rates. 120 FPS is the current gold standard.

- **Wireless:** Is the HMD wireless? Currently the Rift, Vive, and PSVR require a cable from the HMD to the workstation. There are aftermarket options available that can use wireless HMD, but they are not yet ready for the mainstream. This too will likely be an option that differentiates the low and high end HMDs from each manufacturer in the next year or two. Currently, only the HoloLens is wireless with positional tracking.

- **Optics adjustment**: Can the user adjust the optics in their HMD to match their needs? The Gear system allows the user to focus the HMD. The Rift, and Vive, and HoloLens allow for IPD (inter-pupillary distance) adjustment (the distance between the eyes). As HMDs become more mainstream, these may be features that differentiate between the high and low-end systems sold by the same manufacturer.

- **Operating system**: Which operation system is required to run? There is a move afoot for an open standards system that would allow HMDs to work across systems, lowering or removing the current garden walls.

- **Built-in Camera**: Does the HMD have a built-in camera that is accessible? While all smartphones have cameras, only the Gear has apps that make use of that functionality. The Daydream covers the camera. At the moment, only the HoloLens makes frequent use of its built-in camera. But the Vive and Gear could use the camera for some novel UX.

- **AR/VR**: Augmented Reality is projected by many to be a bigger market than virtual reality, though at present, HoloLens is the only mass market AR HMD available.

  The camera in the Vive and Gear could one day be used for more AR apps, in theory. Augmented Reality is projected by many to be a bigger market than Virtual Reality, though at the moment, HoloLens is the only mass market AR HMD available.

- **Natural user interface**: While all of the systems can be modified to include both voice recognition and gesture recognition with add-ons such as Leap Motion, only the HoloLens is built with gesture and voice input as the default input. The voice recognition is part of Windows 10 Cortana, and performs similar. The gesture recognition has only two actual gestures: click (and click and drag) and back.

Primer of best practices

Beyond creating great experiences, the number one goal in VR should be the comfort of the user. Specifically, not making the user feel ill from motion sickness.

Input

In our work, we have found the user interface of the Vive, Oculus, and PSVR to be the most reliable, easiest to train and best suited for fine-tuned gestures and manipulation.

The HoloLens natural input gestures can take a few minutes to learn and the voice recognition, while very reliable, even in noisy conditions, can be tricky due to the nuances of language and the wide ranges of synonyms that exist. Grab/Pinch/Hold/Grasp/Clutch/Seize/Take can all mean the same thing to different users as can Drop/Place/Release/Let Go/Place here. Keeping vocabulary to a minimum while building in as much redundancy as possible is the best design choice.

For Cardboard VR (though it can be used in all the other systems), the most common user interface is simply *gaze select*. The user puts the cross-hair on an icon and holds it there for several seconds. Typically, an animated circle will fill, signifying the action is selected. This is in large part because users need to hold the cardboard devices to their face with both hands. A one-button tap or finger can also be used, but can be unreliable given the rubber band/magnetic/cardboard construction.

In all cases, user fatigue, eye strain, and motion sickness should be included in the design consideration.

Collaboration: While all of the systems can allow for multiple users to interact with the same computer generated imagery, either in the same physical room, or remotely, AR, specifically the HoloLens, allows the user to both see the CGI and the user's face. This can give important non-verbal cues.

Movement

It is best, but not always possible, either due to the distances or the type of HMD used, that the user be in control of movement with a 1 to 1 ratio. That is, if a user walks 1 m, then the world moves with them 1 m. There are situations where this is not exactly possible; a game on a very macro scale where you control planets and stars would not be enjoyable or practical with 1 to 1 moments. The same is true for a game on a micro level, where you need to protect blood cells and destroy cancer cells as you fly though a human body. The movement should at the very least be consistent and relative to the size of the player in their world.

Rapidly moving can quickly create a mismatch between what your eyes are telling you (visual) and what your body is telling you (vestibular and proprioceptive). This mismatch can quickly create motion sickness. Motion sickness is an important design consideration as it doesn't just make a user sick in the short term. The effects can last for hours and the user may have an aversion to your content (or any VR/AR experience) in the future.

It is best to keep the movement slow, steady, and predictable. If large areas need to be traversed quickly, move the user there instantaneously and fade to black in between the old location and the new location. This *teleportation* is the most common form of movement for large distances currently in use. Often the distance the user can move is restricted, not for technical reasons, but to give the user more control and greater accuracy, ensuring that they will move where they are expected to move. Often this distance is represented with an arc, not unlike the user tossing a marker of where they wanted to move to. You can get away with fast movements in your design, if they still enable the player to be in control: a cockpit in a spacecraft, for example.

Make sure that the user maintains control of camera movement. Do not use camera shake as you would in a traditional, non-VR game to add to the illusion of movement, and provide feedback that damage is being taken or the character is waking from a dream. When you take the camera control away from the user, you are dramatically increasing the likelihood that the user will suffer motion sickness. Always keep head tracking enabled once the user begins their VR experience. Don't turn off head tracking, to enable a more traditional gamepad or mouse/keyboard movement scheme. The user will become disorientated.

There is nothing to prevent the player from clipping through the geometry. Regular game collision will not work as the user can keep moving through any object (wall, car, couch, table) that they can reach. However users, especially new users, are very reluctant to move inside of an object that seems to be real, to be solid, even if it is just in VR.

Latency must be optimized. Even slight pauses in rendering can lead to motion sickness. Frame rates should be at 90 FPS for positional tracking (Vive, Rift, PSVR) and 60 FPS for rotational tracking (phone-based systems).

If the user is in a system that does not track them positionally (Cardboard, Gear, Daydream), it is best if they are seated before the experience begins. This will help reconcile the visual cues and vestibular cues. As a bonus, if the chair can spin, it will enhance the experience, and encourage the user to look all the way around.

If the user is near a very large object (iceberg, ship, whale,) that is moving, they may believe they are the one that is moving. Providing sufficient visual cues to drive home the fact that the large object is moving and not the player is key for ensuring that the player does not get motion sickness.

User interface and experience design

In positional tracked systems (Vive, Rift, PSVR, HoloLens), be aware of the fact that users are going to be different heights. Ensure that your experience can accommodate someone who is 1 m and someone who is 2 m tall. If you are going to have the players reach for inventory items, either from a belt attached to the player, or from a table top, design accordingly so that all players can reach them.

Follow some of the old Kinect design best practices. Using your arms with a wireless controller on each hand in VR can be surprisingly fatiguing. This is especially true when the user must hold their arms at full extension. Build rest time into your experiences. Allow the users to assume different poses and relax from time to time. Keep in mind that users may have different levels of conditioning, and what may be an easy experience for a college-age developer, may be a challenging experience for older or differently abled users.

Ensure your users can be aware of their surroundings. Swinging at a virtual ghost can have them banging into a wall, TV, or another guest, damaging themselves, hardware, or others.

Render splash screens and UI in 3D space so that they can move *realistically* as the player expects them to. They need not be built into a *helmet* that they player appears to wear, as many early VR experiences used to; they can be built into the world as if in a Sci-Fi version of a smart assistant.

If you are going to use a *helmet* to project the UI, ensure that the UI elements render in front of everything else, but not so close that it causes extreme, stereoscopic disparity, which can quickly fatigue the user and/or lead to headaches. This may mean that your *helmet* is larger than it would be if it really existed. Stereoscopic 3D is an important cue for 3D space, but it is a rather weak cue and can be overpowered with most 2D cues (occlusion, perspective, and so on).

Keep in mind the display screen is just inches from the user's eyes. Any large change in brightness will be exacerbated and may cause discomfort. Rapidly flashing/flickering images in any display may cause seizures; having flickering displays that take up nearly all of a user's field of view would most likely exacerbate that issue in people who are prone to seizures already.

If it is easy to select a menu option accidentally in VR, ensure the user can quickly and efficiently back out. It is often easy to select an incorrect menu item in VR compared to the accuracy of a mouse and keyboard or game controller. Snapping the user from one input to another is one way to address this concern, as is a confirmation Yes/No screen.

Motion sickness

Why do you get motion (or simulator, or VR) sickness? The short answer is that there is a disconnect between what your body is telling your brain and what your eyes are telling your brain. Your body is telling your brain you are moving (or not moving) while your eyes are telling your brain that you are moving at a different rate or, in a different direction. The effect is not unlike getting seasick on a boat. In VR, you can be sitting still, but the world can be rotating, or you can be walking, but the world can be moving at a different rate or angle. This can cause you to feel ill. Some suggest that to your body, the feelings are similar to being poisoned, so your body tries to get rid of that poison, by vomiting.

The effects seem to be more pronounced in women than in men and seem to grow in intensity as we age. Some argue that this is because the fluid in our inner ear becomes thicker and is less responsive as we age.

Motion sickness prevention, there is no cure

If you are designing VR experiences, you are more likely to suffer from motion sickness for two primary reasons. First, you will be experiencing more time in VR per day than any of your users will experience in a month. Second, these experiences are likely to occur when your experience is not optimized and will have inadequate or inconsistent frame rates.

While there are some foods and acupressure techniques that work to reduce motion sickness symptoms in some people, there is no cure for motion sickness; once it affects you, you cannot take a pill and instantly feel better. As such it is better to know the warning signs and when to stop. If you get a severe case of motion sickness, you may lose an entire day's productivity, as you may very well not feel up to programming.

To prevent motion sickness, take regular breaks. Every 10-15 minutes is a common recommendation. You may want to design your VR experiences to have levels with this duration in mind. At least, design save points to fit this benchmark to give your users an opportunity to rest.

If you begin to feel sick, stop. You can't power through it. Trying to do so will just make it worse, not better.

Closing your eyes in VR is your best defense against motion sickness. If something is making you feel uncomfortable, uneasy, or sick, then close your eyes. Especially if it is a cut scene or some other action where you can't control your viewpoint. If it is a situation where you must maintain visual attention (say in a flight simulator), focus on one point and track that one point until the camera returns to a more normal position. Or, especially in a flight sim, tilt your head to match the tilt of the horizon in the VR experience. It will help to a degree.

If you do suffer from motion sickness:

- Sit down and move your head as little as possible.
- Close your eyes.
- When you feel well enough to move, get up and walk around, outside if possible, somewhere with a clear view to the horizon.

Food: while the empirical evidence isn't strong, there is no downside to eating ginger (ginger ale, ginger candy, candied ginger, pickled ginger), and it must work for some people to be such a common recommendation for seasickness. If you are prone to VR sickness, do your best to avoid spicy, greasy, cabbage-laden foods before you enter VR. But be sure to drink plenty of water.

A low or inconsistent frame rate is the most reliable way to make you sick. You may need a faster video card, faster CPU, or better optimization in your code, or cleaner, lower poly art assets, fewer particle effects, less accurate physics simulation, and so on.

P-6 pressure point: The seasickness bands work by applying pressure to the pericardium acupressure point, which relieves motion sickness in some users. If you do not have a band, you can massage the area yourself and see if that alleviates the symptoms.

Turn your hand palm side up, and using the thumb from your other hand, place it down one inch from the bottom on your palm. You should feel two tendons at the base of your palm. Massage that point with light pressure, then switch to the other hand. It doesn't work for everyone, but it is worth trying.

Many people report hot flushes as they progress into VR sickness. If you do get sick, try some cold air, a walk outside, or a cold towel on your head.

Other Books You May Enjoy

If you enjoyed this book, you may be interested in these other books by Packt:

Augmented Reality for Developers
Jonathan Linowes, Krystian Babilinski

ISBN: 978-1-78728-643-6

- Build Augmented Reality applications through a step-by-step, tutorial-style project approach
- Use the Unity 3D game engine with the Vuforia AR platform, open source ARToolKit, Microsoft's Mixed Reality Toolkit, Apple ARKit, and Google ARCore, via the C# programming language
- Implement practical demo applications of AR including education, games, business marketing, and industrial training
- Employ a variety of AR recognition modes, including target images, markers, objects, and spatial mapping
- Target a variety of AR devices including phones, tablets, and wearable smartglasses, for Android, iOS, and Windows HoloLens
- Develop expertise with Unity 3D graphics, UIs, physics, and event systems
- Explore and utilize AR best practices and software design patterns

Getting Started with React VR

John Gwinner

ISBN: 978-1-78847-660-7

- Use Blender 2.79 to make virtual reality objects for Web VR
- Import free models into VR and how to include those in your code
- Build a Virtual Museum with interactive art pieces
- Create your first VR App and customizing it
- Build animations by procedurally changing an object's position, using timers and Animated APIs
- Incorporate React Native code and JavaScript code in your VR world

Leave a review - let other readers know what you think

Please share your thoughts on this book with others by leaving a review on the site that you bought it from. If you purchased the book from Amazon, please leave us an honest review on this book's Amazon page. This is vital so that other potential readers can see and use your unbiased opinion to make purchasing decisions, we can understand what our customers think about our products, and our authors can see your feedback on the title that they have worked with Packt to create. It will only take a few minutes of your time, but is valuable to other potential customers, our authors, and Packt. Thank you!

Index

Made in the USA
Middletown, DE
25 July 2018